A MINNESOTA REMEMBRANCE:
The Kelly Field Mister,
the Schoolmarm,
Politics and Twilight

VOLUME FOUR

The old Main Drive Camp turned Nelson's Camp, a fishing and hunting resort near the mouth of the Prairie

Robert O. Harder

Published by the
Aitkin County Historical Society
Aitkin, Minnesota

River at Big Sandy Lake. Fishing boats stand ready below the steps that lead up to the camp.

Please direct all correspondence and book orders to:
Director
Aitkin County Historical Society
P.O. Box 215
Aitkin, MN 56431

ISBN 0-9665976-4-8

Published by the Aitkin County Historical Society

Printed in the United States of America

INTRODUCTION

In this, the fourth and final volume in the series, we find the Marcus Nelsons picking up the pieces from their 1926 bankruptcy. Marcus buries himself in real estate work, managing to keep the Tamarack store and Nelson-Heller Co. limping along. Mamie does house cleaning and ekes out a few dollars with her art. Myrtle blossoms into a vivacious, independent woman and attends Duluth State Teachers College. After teaching for one year, she decides to try something else. A few years later, however, the Depression is at its height, and she has no choice but to return to the classroom. She is pleasantly surprised by how much she enjoys the work and settles into a teaching career. Orvis, who has in every way developed into a Golden Boy, is captivated by Charles Lindbergh's Atlantic flight in May, 1927, even more so because the Lindbergh and Nelson families are acquainted. He enlists in the Army, later attending the world-famous Army flying school at Kelly Field, Texas, marking the beginning of a sparkling aviation career.

Although Marcus and Mamie had contrived to get a jump on the Depression in 1926, the rest of the country caught up with them in 1930. Times are very hard; anyone with any kind of a job at all is quite fortunate. By 1934, the economic and political climate in Minnesota is so radicalized, Marcus senses an opportunity in politics. He is elected a Minnesota State Representative and becomes an active participant in the weightiest issues of the day--unemployment, real estate tax burdens, the question of a sales tax, the socialist/communist movement, and social security. But the times are so contentious and the problems so seemingly insoluble, the political winds continue their pattern of changing every two years. Marcus is retired by the voters in November, 1936, and he attempts to re-enter the business world. But his many personal, financial, and health problems mount, threatening both his marriage and his own life.

Washburn Hall
Duluth State Teachers College
November 12th, 1925

Mama,

Your darling daughter is in disgrace! Your box arrived this afternoon so Rose and I got the brilliant idea of having the girls in tonight for a feed. In order to get a thrill out of it we planned to have it after 10:00. So Rose bought pickles, etc. and I furnished apples & crackers. Everything went fine for half an hour then some of the kids thought they heard Mrs. Jones coming so they ducked all over the place. They made such a racket getting under beds, etc. that the housekeeper came up. Laina Alatalo saw her coming & told us & a lot of the kids to beat it. The rest of us didn't believe her as she is always saying something like that for fun. Mrs. Flaherty opened the door & bawled us out to a fare-ye-well. I sat on the bed with my mouth open & gaped. All of the girls were hidden but Lynette & Acktie & of course Rose and I. Mrs. Flaherty went down & told Mrs. Jones & just as the girls were going here came the boss herself. Acktie bumped into her in the hall. "Pay me a quarter in the morning," said Mrs. J. Hazel, a girl who wasn't in on it, came out in the hall to see what the racket was about and Mrs. Jones told her to pay a quarter, too. I'm going to tell Mrs. J. in morning that Hazel wasn't there. Then she came to our door and said, "Myrtle." I said, "Yes, Mrs. Jones" in a scared voice. "Who were the girls who were in here?" Boy! I was scared. I said, "I can't remember who all was in here." I didn't want to tell on the girls. "Tell them all to pay me a quarter in the morning," she said. So you see I'm going to be a quarter poorer in the morning. It was kind of fun, it was so exciting, but I can't afford such expensive excitement anymore. Rose and I went to bed, but were too breathless to sleep so I am writing to you and Rose is studying.

Are you ashamed of me? Hope not. It was such a lot of fun - while it lasted.

Will you send me a pair of Black Silk stockings sometime soon? I'd like them to be as nice as you can get at the store. Be sure they're black. Thanks for the dollar.

Myrtle

P.S. Fri. morning. We went down & paid our fines this a.m. Ten of us went at once. Mrs. Jones had to laugh at us. She wasn't a bit mad. Said, "Kind of expensive isn't it?" Then she said, "Better do your eating weekends after this." We all laughed.

Myrtle

Washburn Hall
Feb 28, 1926

Dearest Mother,

If you see Dad or know where to find him please tell him that I must have my board money immediately. It was supposed to have been paid yesterday. Don't know what they'll do to me if it isn't paid at once. I've written and written but I suppose he didn't get the letters somehow.

Guess you better send me some more bread if you can. It's so good I've been eating a lot. Put in some peanuts if you have room.

We are to have spare ribs and cabbage tonight. I love 'em but the ribs we get here are usually pretty spare.

Please if you know how to get hold of Dad remind him about my money as I've got to have it tomorrow. I'm getting nervous prostration worrying about money.

Myrtle

P.S. Later. Rose just dropped off a letter from Dad with my money. Whew!

1

During the previous winter of 1925, Orvis attended
Hamline College in St. Paul for one semester.

Washburn Hall
April 30, 1926

Mom,

I went to the Darling Observatory last night with about 30 school girls. We wanted to see the Moon through the big telescope, but it went behind the clouds and stayed there. Mr. Darling took us to the office and showed some slides and lectured on them. From the looks of things I've come to the conclusion that the Man in the Moon had a bad case of Smallpox. Wouldn't you know the bloomin' thing came out bright and full just as we were getting home!

I applied to schools in Aitkin, Cass, Itasca, and Isanti counties. I want a school so badly and I know I can do a lot better than a lot of these kids. Just because I haven't been teaching for forty years is no sign that I can't, if I get a chance.

Myrtle

3315 Hennepin Ave. So. Mpls
Fri 14 May 26

My Darling Son Orvis,

Dad says hello & hopes all goes well at Tamarack. He and Martin may have something for you this fall on a new lake shore deal over to Gull Lake. He will write you when he feels better, he's pretty punk at the moment. Is planning on fishing after he gets home till he regains his health from the Mastoid poisoning.

Your Loving Mother

Washburn Hall
May 17, 1926

Orv,

We girls went down to the dock to see Evelyn off this morning. The street car conductor told us to get off at 5th Ave West. That turned out to be the ferry dock. Then a man there sent us way off to the freight docks. By the time we finally found the right dock, the boat was just leaving so I didn't get to see Evelyn at all. We went out on the light house by the Aerial Bridge and watched the boats go through. I've got huge blisters on my heels from running around so much looking for the dock.

Too bad Grandpa Mayhall died. Irlene Kelley wrote that the trio at the service was wonderful. Wish I could have heard you.

Write again. I like your letters.

Myrtle

P.S. It's Dad's birthday tomorrow. Better write him a letter as I expect he is down in the dumps from his health and money worries. I guess he aims to stick to real estate from now on.

TEACHER'S CONTRACT

This Agreement made this **Eighth day of July 1926** between Grandy School District No. 58 in the County of Isanti and State of Minnesota, by the School Board, and Myrtle Nelson, a legally qualified teacher in ungraded elementary public schools. The said Myrtle Nelson shall teach the school for the term of nine months for the sum of One Hundred Dollars per month commencing on a certain date of August, 1926.

School Board agrees to keep the school house and premises in good repair, furnish suitable and sufficient fuel, provide janitor work, be prepared for fire, and to supply to the school room textbooks, maps, stationery, and other articles necessary for carrying out desired work.

Be it noted there shall be a Potato Vacation during which time Myrtle Nelson shall receive no pay.

    O.J. Engstrom
    Chairman, School Board

MINNESOTA
COMMON SCHOOL CERTIFICATE
FIRST GRADE
ISSUED UPON COMPLETION OF ONE YEAR OF PROFESSIONAL TRAINING
FOR RURAL SCHOOL TEACHERS IN A STATE TEACHERS COLLEGE

THIS CERTIFIES THAT *Myrtle B. Nelson*

is a high school graduate and in addition has completed one year of the required professional training in the State Teachers College at *Duluth* Minnesota, has furnished evidence of skill and good moral character, and is hereby entitled to this FIRST GRADE CERTIFICATE, which, when signed and recorded by a County Superintendent, qualifies the holder to teach in the ungraded elementary public schools of Minnesota for *two* YEARS from the date hereof.

This certificate is *not* valid in Graded Elementary Schools.

Saint Paul, Minnesota *August 1* 1926

J. M. McConnell
Commissioner of Education.

Eveline Judin
County Superintendent of Schools.

Isanti, County, Minnesota.

Mpls
Aug 5th, 1926

Folks,

Elsie Borg and I went to a concert at Lake Harriet last night. The players from the Orpheum were out there and gave short skits. We had seen 'em once so I guess we enjoyed them more than the rest. We had a community sing afterwards which was broadcast. Of course, we yelled our loudest for our first radio appearance. Plus a couple of giggles. The singing must have sounded comic over the radio. It seemed pretty weak to us in the audience. I talked a lot with one of the players. He had a big open car and took the whole gang home afterward!

    Myrtle

We are out for a Joy Ride.

3

First Nat'l Bank of Aitkin
Aug 22, 1926

Marcus,

Paul Heller was here representing Nelson-Heller Co. We signed a lease that will allow you to continue to operate the store, and provide us with some sort of tangible return on the asset. As you pointed out, there is no one better to run the thing & it would do little good for either of us to let the place rot.

I sincerely hope you & Paul can make a go of it.

B.R. Hassman, Cashier

P.S. I never felt as bad at a foreclosure as I did at yours.

Grandy, Minn.
Aug 23rd, 1926

Myrtle Dear,

I hope to get a chance to get down to Mpls to see you before you leave for here. Maybe I can manage a few hours and we will each buy a mink coat or a pair of ermine wristlets or something. (Audience please politely sneeze, giggle, choke, or just laugh).

Yes, you are right about my Joe. He is exactly like a race horse when it comes to shopping. He gallops madly from one place to another and always drives you crazy telling you to hurry. Then when he gets into a music store you can wait and wait and wait 'till the parasite mosses grow on your whiskers, and you feel old and gnarled when you come out.

Oh dearie, I haven't so much hope for selling my book. I had intended improving it this summer but never touched it. This will be its third trip. Costs like the devil to mail 'em.

If it comes right down to it I can earn a good living writing for pulp paper magazines - lots do it. I met a girl who just writes true confessions. And there is a man in St. Paul who writes and sells westerns all the time. I'd hate to tho because I like to get a little pleasure out of writing and being myself - but believe me if I ever start writing about Six Gun Lucas or Laments of Red Light Annie, my name isn't going to be tacked on the stories - not by a long shot.

I have a Thesaurus now - have you ever used one? It has all words & expressions grouped. But they are expensive. All I need now is a quiet wholesome place & a big table, and someone to bring me my meals! Also paper, pen, etc. Say kiddo, are you still "scribblin?"

Enough already. I must oil up my Palmer & get to work.

Carol Newman

P.S. By the way - they are not teaching Palmer in Isanti. Using the Laurel system instead. Well kiddo, here comes your first teaching term!

MINNEAPOLIS JOURNAL
Sunday, October 10, 1926

TINGDALE URGES ADVERTISING MINNESOTA'S 10,000 LAKES BY SLOGAN ON ALL CAR LICENSES

Minnesota is missing a wonderful opportunity of advertising it's 10,000 lakes, according to Warren Tingdale, manager of Tingdale Bros. & son of it's founder, who would have the license tags of the more than 2,000,000 automobiles owned here bear an inscription.

"Every year hundreds of thousands of cars are driven out of Minnesota and everyone is a potential advertiser of the wonderful merits of the state as a summer recreation ground," Mr. Tingdale explained.

"Florida has used somewhat the same idea in carrying a map of the state on the license tag. I intend proposing to state officials that the license plates for next year have the words 'Land of 10,000 Lakes' printed below the numbers."

As it looked in 1911. There appears to be
a beached wanigan in the background.

Mpls
Dec 19, 1926

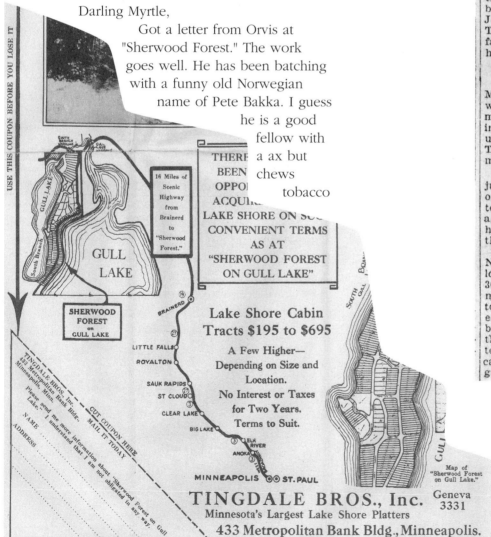

Darling Myrtle,
    Got a letter from Orvis at "Sherwood Forest." The work goes well. He has been batching with a funny old Norwegian name of Pete Bakka. I guess he is a good fellow with a ax but chews tobacco

THERE HAS BEEN NO OPPORTUNITY TO ACQUIRE LAKE SHORE ON SUCH CONVENIENT TERMS AS AT "SHERWOOD FOREST ON GULL LAKE"

16 Miles of Scenic Highway from Brainerd to "Sherwood Forest."

GULL LAKE

SHERWOOD FOREST on GULL LAKE

BRAINERD
LITTLE FALLS
ROYALTON
SAUK RAPIDS
ST CLOUD
CLEAR LAKE
BIG LAKE
ELK RIVER
ANOKA
MINNEAPOLIS ST. PAUL

USE THIS COUPON BEFORE YOU LOSE IT

TINGDALE BROS., Inc.
433 Metropolitan Bank Bldg.,
Minneapolis, Minn.
Please send me more information about "Sherwood Forest on Gull Lake." I understand that I am not obligated in any way.

NAME
ADDRESS

CUT COUPON HERE — MAIL IT TODAY

Lake Shore Cabin
Tracts $195 to $695

A Few Higher—
Depending on Size and
Location.
No Interest or Taxes
for Two Years.
Terms to Suit.

Map of
"Sherwood Forest
on Gull Lake."

TINGDALE BROS., Inc.
Minnesota's Largest Lake Shore Platters
433 Metropolitan Bank Bldg., Minneapolis.
Geneva
3331

"South Branch, Gull Lake" is now known as Lake Margaret.

all the time and don't talk. Has a permanent stoop from so many years as a ox man. ha. ha. Your Pa was out there and had to stay a week

to teach Orvis how to cook, Pete can't and Orvis was poor at it.

Your Father did not get his money back and borrowed some of me. He cannot get it into his head a man cannot act as banker for all his friends. I told him I needed a new hat and coat so he said he would get them.

Mom

P.S. They were quite proud of Orvis at Tingdale office for selling that Gull Lake lot.

Orvis (L) and Pete Bakka in their shack. Note Orvis is pulling on a string that he has rigged to trip the camera shutter.

Martinsville, Indiana
Dec 21, 1926

Cousin Myrtle,

Hope you are teaching lots of important things to the Grandy little ones. Do you like it there? Your last letter sounded like you had been happier.

Say, how is that beaux of yours? You will have to keep me informed. Now don't you go and jump the broomstick! Ha! Ha!

I must tell you a little dirty joke but don't you dare tell anyone I told you. Do you remember reading about Browning, the real old fellow who married the young flapper peaches. Well, do you know why she laid on her back in the sand? To keep her bottom from Browning.

Carroll Pitcher

Mpls
Sat Mar 5-27

Mr. O. Nelson
Pequot, Minn.
C/O Mr. McClintock at Gull Lake
My dear Son,

Myrtle came last nite, rode down with garageman. She has decided she is not going to sign a contract at Grandy for next year. She is getting sick of all guys up there seems like. Well, don't get "entangled" with anyone till you are old enough, for if you are like most of my people we mature rather slow. Is best way too for usually I notice they are smarter.

Ben Finch and Dad are together working at office. Was there and got $10 but had to give him 3 he had borrowed off someone.

Is a big card party going on next door and you can be glad you are not home. 6 tables, that makes 24. Gab. Gab. Gab.

Myrtle says she wants to go to Ind. as soon as school is out. Why don't you come along with us?

From your Mother.

Met Bank Bldg, Mpls
March 15, 1927

Son:

Regards the corduroy road, use all the poplar you can get on the road, regardless of size. Lay out the good 16 foot poles that are say from 3 inches up, and put in a couple of tiers of these on top. This will solve the problem of getting the timber you need.

Of course, you will need to hire a team, and anyone that owns any kind of horses would not want every Tom, Dick, and Harry to drive them for him - so go ahead and hire a team and teamster whenever you need them.

In regards to the house logs, I think your judgment will be alright on this. I want you to keep in mind that we want nice, straight, good sized building logs for this main cabin that we are going to build up there.

I think it is your 20th birthday in a few days and I want to congratulate you, and hope that you will get bigger and better all the time. Your Mother is sending a package to you by parcel post to-day, and when you get this, I know we will be able to read your letters without calling in all the foreigners to figure out what you are trying to tell us. When you write by hand, don't be quite so quick on the trigger.

"Dad"

Met Bank Bldg
March 25, 1927

Son:

Get the rest of the work done soon as possible, so we can get the stakes set. We should have all the logs piled up so it looks like business. Do a good job so that when Mr. Martin and R.T. Tingdale get

```
                              Pequot, Minn.
                              April 4, 1927
Dear Mom:
         Your letter that you wrote last Friday came this
morning. Dad brought the Sunday papers and I notice that
there's a section devoted to Ford advertising. It stated that
no change in price was contemplated. I'll bet that they change them
if that series of adds bring no results. By the time I get ready
to buy we'll probably know. I may buy a Chev. if there seems
to be considerable work in sight.

         Dad also brought my high top shoes. They certainly
put a dandy sole on them. I'm certainly glad that you dug them
out and had dad fix them. Yes, I received my coat. I wrote
Aunt Kate and I thought that I wrote you about them.

         We've certainly had some real feeds the last two days.
I made a double boiler out of two different sized kettles and
some wire. I made a hanger out of the wire and nested the
smaller one in the larger one. It certainly tasted fine.
Jimmy McClintick had supper again with us tonight. I filled
his bowl up several times and was filling mine up again, scraping
the kettle, when he stuck his bowl over and told me to put
some of that in his, that I needn't take it all. Jimmy is Six.
His dad just came down after him, but he's sat down and is
taking it easy.

         It has been raining hard all day. We done  a little
work this morning, but we've been sitting around most of the
day. I've been working spasmodically on a bunch of time order
sheets.
         Pete just pulled a good one. He was talking about
those fat salesmen "sitting around the office waiting for
fish to bite".
         Went over to see the schoolma'am last night. We made
a big batch of fudge. Jones came down to the cabin and sat
around for an hour or so this afternoon. He said that time
was dragging pretty hard on him. He's such a hard worker that
he don't know what to do with himself when he can't.
         Next time Dad goes, go along. It only costs a little
more to sleep two than one and a person has to eat where ever
they are. It would do you a lot of good to get out. Gosh, I'd
be dead if I'd have stayed in that city as long as you have.
         It still is raining hard. I hope it clears up a
little by morning. When work stops, pay stops, and a person
goes right on eating up the profits.
         Well, so long,
                              Orvis
```

up there, they will appreciate that you fellows have not been stalling around and killing time. We want to be ready this spring when the buyers start arriving.

Dad

Trafalgar, Ind.
May 26, 1927

Dad,

Mama and Orvis are out taking Grandpa Barnett for a ride, and I am home enjoying this gorgeous day, so nice after a cold Minnesota winter. Charlie called & said he was going to take me to the Auto Races in Indianapolis. I'm so tickled because I wanted to go so badly. Expect I will have plenty to tell in my next letter.

Orvis is full of the Lindbergh flight to Paris. He tells everyone he runs into that he is friends with him. Wasn't it just that one time when you and Mr. Lindbergh took the boys fishing? Orv has gotten airplane crazy, talks about flying all the time. He has heard that Army men get preference to flying schools if they don't have the 2 years of college, so he is talking about enlisting in the Air Corps! Mama hasn't said anything one way or the other.

Myrtle

P.S. I want to look for work down here, as I have nothing doing up home. Mama said all right with her if you do not object.

First Nat'l Bank of Aitkin
June 9, 1927

Marcus & Mamie,

We have matters in hand pertaining to your re-purchase of the 8 acre Drive Camp site at Prairie River, Sandy Lake. I am assigning a Mortgage Deed to you in consideration of $1,200 received from Mr. Martin Tingdale. He will hold the Warranty Deed until such time as he has received payment in full from you.

Ben Hassman

Mpls
Aug 4th, 1927

Wife & Kids:

Haven't heard from you for some time so do not know if you are coming or going. Is Orvis & Myrtle going to stay in Indiana?

We will have to sign a new lease or move Sept 1st. I don't know what you want to do. I must know

what you expect to do as the landlord is anxious to know.

Marcus

Mpls
Aug 10, 1927

Wife:

Rec. your letter today that you are coming home also consent for Orvis to join the Army Air Corps for 3 years. I mailed this out today properly signed. Understand he is to be at Fort Benjamin Harrison on the 12th.

Hope now that he started he will make good, and also be careful. He should make good as he has a good Brain and Body. I hope you never regret encouraging this.

Things are slow here but hope it gets better. I am starting today on straight comm. so will be up against an uncertain condition, but will have to make it go.

Marcus

P.S. You did not say but I guess Myrtle is staying.

Indianapolis
Sunday Aug 14, 1927

Mother and Dad,

Aunt Dilla has put me up in a spare bedroom and it has taken me all day to get settled in. I haven't a job yet. Wassons and Ayres told me they'd be taking on their help about Sept 1st.

Orvis got orders to proceed by rail to Chanute Field, Rantoul, Ill. for assignment as a student at the Air Corps Technical School. It's over by Urbana, not so far away from here.

I cashed a $20 check last night and had my hair cut. Looks real spurious. Whatever that means.

Love, Myrtle

P.S. I'll need some money if I can't find a job soon.

Indypls
Aug 22, 1927

Mother & Dad,

No luck yet. I am running an ad in tomorrow's paper. If you can send a couple of dollars it will help like everything.

Dutch was over Sat. night, but I ditched him and went with a fellow that had a Marmon touring. He's more fun too.

Myrtle

8

Chanute Field
Rantoul, Illinois
Sun Aug 28, 1927

Mom,

Have been so busy ever since I got here. Seems we are either drilling or working every waking minute. I get K.P. a lot, just got off & will scratch a few lines before bed. Awful tired.

I think they are going to give me what I wanted - the ground and aerial photographic course. Next class won't start for week - ten days so expect will get more of same till then. Would like to get out of this K.P. business.

Orv

Chanute Field
Sept 6, 1927

Mom,

I'm a prison guard now. We follow them around all day while they work. I'd rather do something else

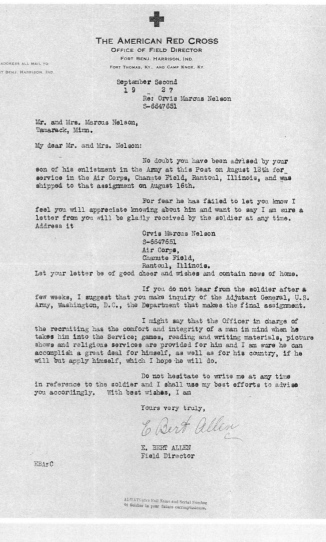

THE AMERICAN RED CROSS
OFFICE OF FIELD DIRECTOR
FORT BENJ. HARRISON, IND.
FORT THOMAS, KY., AND CAMP KNOX, KY.

ADDRESS ALL MAIL TO
FORT BENJ. HARRISON, IND.

September Second
19 ___ 27
Re: Orvis Marcus Nelson
S-6647651

Mr. and Mrs. Marcus Nelson,
Tamarack, Minn.

My dear Mr. and Mrs. Nelson:

No doubt you have been advised by your son of his enlistment in the Army at this Post on August 12th for service in the Air Corps, Chanute Field, Rantoul, Illinois, and was shipped to that assignment on August 16th.

For fear he has failed to let you know I feel you will appreciate knowing about him and want to say I am sure a letter from you will be gladly received by the soldier at any time. Address it

Orvis Marcus Nelson
S-6647651
Air Corps,
Chanute Field,
Rantoul, Illinois.

Let your letter be of good cheer and wishes and contain news of home.

If you do not hear from the soldier after a few weeks, I suggest that you make inquiry of the Adjutant General, U.S. Army, Washington, D.C., the Department that makes the final assignment.

I might say that the Officer in charge of the recruiting has the comfort and integrity of a man in mind when he takes him into the Service; games, reading and writing materials, picture shows and religious services are provided for him and I am sure he can accomplish a great deal for himself, as well as for his country, if he will but apply himself, which I hope he will do.

Do not hesitate to write me at any time in reference to the soldier and I shall use my best efforts to advise you accordingly. With best wishes, I am

Yours very truly,

E. Bert Allen

E. BERT ALLEN
Field Director

EBArC

ALWAYS give Full Name and Serial Number
of Soldier in your future correspondence.

Headquarters, Chanute Field.

but they are the boss. Our orders are to shoot to kill if they try to get away. They say if one escapes on your watch you have to serve their sentence out but don't know if that is so or not. We have a .45 automatic, carry it in a holster on right hip, and a sawed-off shotgun. I have to work nearly as hard as the prisoners following them around & then the mental strain you're under is not inconsiderable. Between guarding and bugling I get out of K.P. though & that is not so bad.

Orv

Private Orvis Nelson

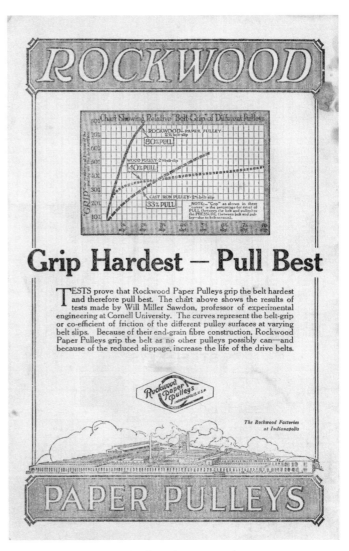

Myrtle finally got a job...

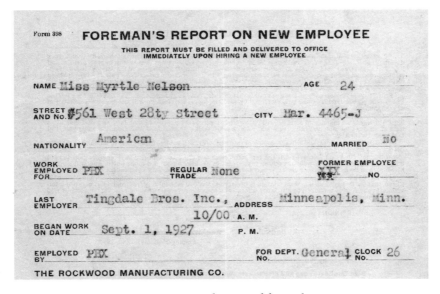

...running the switchboard.

Big Sandy Lake
Sept 9-27

Girlie,

So glad about your new job. It is always a relief to know you can pay your own way.

You remember Myrtle that city fellow Fuzzy White who used to hunt ducks here years ago. Well guess who showed up. Had a fellow name of Baldwin with him. They staid for supper & hinted around long enough till I finally put them up in the shack. This Baldwin is so nervous of wild animals he don't sleep good nites and Dad & Dennis don't help much telling tales. It's funny. I guess I told too many too, not knowing he was timid. Geo. Steffer was up and scared him last night scratching on screen. Carr agreed to wear Dad's coat and play beast but went back on it afraid he'd get scared too bad. Fuzzy is having a fine time and is very deaf & don't seem to appreciate his friend's predicament. Baldwin ready to leave at drop of hat. ha. Guess us country folks are easily entertained.

Mom

P.S. Went to a craw dad hole and got clay to fix my fireplace. Looks fine.

Indypls
Sept 15th, 1927

Mother & Dad,

I had a hard day today and am kind of blue I guess. It's been terribly lonely since Eldra got married. She was so much fun and had so many friends. I wouldn't meet anybody in a thousand years if I had to depend on this Rockwood outfit. They're a bunch of old fogies. These kids are either out with their men or dead to the world.

I certainly work my head off for $14 a week, but I like it better than teaching school. If I knew somebody so evenings wouldn't be lonesome I wouldn't mind such low wages.

Myrtle

Chanute Field
Sept. 30, 1927

Mom,

I moved to Photo Section yesterday. We start on Monday with Mathematics and Theoretical Photography. Am on bugling today. Don't mind it anymore, got over the buck fever stage.

I'm glad you and Dad have moved into your log cabin. It's too cold to stay in that drafty old Cook Shanty. I'd like to be there for a week but I expect it'll be a long, long time before I see that country again.

One of my prisoners told me sometime back that when he got out he was going to look me up and beat me up. He got out yesterday & I looked him up today & asked him if he was looking for me. No, he said, he wasn't trying to find me.

Con mucho gusto,
Orvis

Chanute Field
Sun Oct 9, 1927

Mom,

Note you say in your last letter I've evaded answering your questions as to church. As a rule, I go every Sunday. I've went a couple of times to the Christian Church here also the Methodist and then the Chapel here on the field.

We had quite a review yesterday. Lasted over an hour. One of the platoons balled things up so we had to go thru it again. I enjoyed it myself though, so I didn't mind at all. They certainly are interesting and, to an outsider, thrilling. Of course, we don't look so war-like as infantry, for we have no guns, but it is pretty good just the same.

I haven't heard from Dad for quite awhile but expect he is running all over the country as usual. Hello to Carr. Glad your garden on the hill did so well. Are there a lot of ducks in the bay?
Orvis

Indypls
10/17/27

Mom & Dad,

Carroll Pitcher and I went to the Minnesota-Indiana football game Saturday. It seemed so good to see some kids from home! The game ended with the score 14:14. Minnesota was on the way to another score when the whistle blew. Just our luck!

I have everyone here at home and at the office talking football, and listening in on the games. I wish I could go to more of them, but altogether I spent nearly my whole weeks wages on the game Sat,. and it was worth it at any price, but I don't suppose I can do it again for awhile.

I haven't heard from Orvis all week. Guess I'll have to send him some more fudge, so that he'll have to write and thank me. I can't afford to buy the sugar tho I am afraid I will do it anyway.

Our office manager said that I was a hard worker, so I guess I must be doing all right. I worked overtime to make up for the time I took off Saturday so that I wouldn't get docked. Wish I could spend a week just running around for a change. Guess I'm getting lazy. Did I hear you say "getting?" Well, the office gang doesn't think I am lazy, so maybe there is hope yet.

The radio is going. The city mission broadcasted a sermon and some music tonight.

Myrtle

P.S. I know a good new way to put a wave in, Mom. You soak linseed in water, then wet the hair with the water, and put the wave in. The linseed water holds the wave in place until the hair dries.

Enlisted Men's barracks.

Chanute Field
Oct 30, 1927

Mom,

You needn't bother to send along any writing paper as I can get all I could haul in a truck for nothing. But see if you can find my English book. Also a U.S. History. I need palmolive soap, a tube of shaving cream, and another of toothpaste.

We mixed up various kinds of chemicals this afternoon - different developers for different types of negatives. That stuff is hard on the hands. We had optics this morning - that's the science of lenses.

Glad your stone fireplace at the cabin draws so well. That is the most difficult part to build and you surely did it right. I'll bet it feels good to sit in front of it on frosty nights.

Myrtle wrote she went to a Halloween party dressed up in Johnny Hamilton's clown suit. It was too big even for him so that must have been some sight. They took flash light pictures of everyone and she will send you one if they turn out.

Orv

Chanute Field
Dec 1, 1927

Hello Myrtle,

We started Ground Photography today. Lots of ships coming and going on the field. They still have got the prisoners chopping up the old World War Jennies. Awful to see but that's the way they do things here.

Pay day, and the crap & poker games are in full swing - will end in a day or two when the boys are cleaned out. I celebrated with eggs and honest to God fried spuds, with onions. I culled the onions out.

Red Gillette and I took in a show "The Blood Ship." Was better than some others I could mention that were more advertised.

Orv

Grandy, Minn.
Dec 20 1927

My Gawd Moitie,

But it is ages since I've written you. Your letter has utterly shamed me into writing back instanter. I just finished a stack of report cards as high as a house and I feel mighty relieved.

I'm still frost bitten from a trip yesterday. It surely was colder than a step mother's kiss and of

12

course I was sparsely covered in "de feet" by stylish galoshes, and by golly I think I'm going to have chilblains in my ankles. So you can see the kind of a red hot mamma I am - no danger of any moustaches being singed by my hot lips.

Say Myrtle, just how do people cultivate "It" and how can you tell whether they've got "It" or not? I'm examining all the people I know to see if they have "It" but so far I haven't found any examples.

Johnny L. stays in the house now too. Room next to mine. I always go to bed real early because I fear if I came up late I might get into the wrong pew. However, I don't think he has the sex appeal that Eric has - especially when he dances.

Oh yes, Roger M. had his tonsils and adenoids out and Good Night! you'd hardly know the kid. Not that his looks are improved but his mentality is advancing at at least 20 per. Bobby only got 9th in Declamation, which was better than nothing at all. He couldn't do anything when all the noise was going on and everyone moving around. Next time I train one I'll take him to a boiler factory to practice. It doesn't seem right they have to declame under such circumstances, does it?

If you could see the way I'm balancing this paper on one knee! I'm scared the pen might break thru if I press too hard and write on my red flannels.

Mr. & Mrs. Vic Nelson now occupy your old bedroom while Vic puts in bath fixtures. But unless he gets some heat (and some d--n hot heat too) when he goes to take a bath after the first splash

Nelson's Store in 1928. The addition on the right housed Marcus' office. Several businesses in Tamarack were selling gasoline by this time.

Tamarack in 1928.
(L to R) Blue Parrot Koffee and Kandy Kitchen (formerly the Beanery),
Cayo/Cyrus livery and then garage, Erline Kelley's Cash Store
(formerly the Post Office) & McDonald's Store.

he'll be ice cicles.

Bang! Bang! Johnny has fallen out of bed I think by the thump. I must run and get the fire department or something to the rescue.

Your former partner in crime,
Carol Newman

13

Mpls
Jan 9-28

Darling Myrtle,

Dad & I got back O.K. and had an awful good time in Ind. He is full of business and pep like he used to be. Hope he stays that way. Things aren't so good at Tamarack.

You asked about your cold. Keep on putting vix on nite and morning and be careful of drafts.

Orvis sent some wonderful pictures he made by glass, by some system of printing thro a distorting looking glass. Dad is wild over them. The kid knows so much more about cameras than I ever hoped to.

Dad does not like this flat. He wanted his own bath. I told him that at the time but was so cold he did not want to look any longer. They are careless about fires here, let die at nite even the cold nites, and that is not a way to save fuel.

The winters are so hard on me. I hope I do not have any serious trouble.

Mom

Chanute Field
Feb 19, 1928

Folks,

Finished up copying, filters, and lantern slide making Friday. Mosaics tomorrow & for two months.

Arali is whanging away on his rubberneck organ. He gets a spasm now and then.

You should see my moustache! I've got six days in it. I'll let it grow awhile and then whack it. Really should let it go till we go home on furlough. Guess I won't tho might get run out of town. I don't want that to happen. I'm going to do some stepping out tho. Have to take all the girls in the country out stepping. I suppose you'll be in agony, Mom. Well, don't worry. I'll be free, white, & 21 & not nearly as susceptible as I once was. I'm in no hurry. A woman is too much of a bother now, especially when one doesn't want any.

Orv

Chanute Field
Mar 27, 1928

Folks,

The Personnel Office gave out the assignments today. Yes - I got the Philippines. I very nearly burst out the walls of the darkroom with an outbreak of exultation. I will leave right after I get back from furlough.

One more washed out today, so that leaves only six of us left out of the 18 that started.

My furlough starts Sunday 1st of April, so I will soon be on my way home. I hope you can move up to the lake at least while I'm there. Don't worry, I will haul all the water & wood you need. We will get the place nice & toasty.

Orv

Chanute Field
Sun April 15, 1928

Folks,

Am all fresh from my trip home and set to leave on the train for N.Y. tomorrow at 1:25. We are to take the U.S.A.T. (United States Army Transport) Chateau Thierry from New York through the Panama Canal & up to San Francisco. From there we sail across the Pacific (via Hawaii) on the U.S.A.T. U.S. Grant.

I got my extra junk all packed to send to Tamarack. I couldn't get it all in the grip so I'll express the rest in a package. Better retire that grip, I picked it up and the handle broke off. I roped her up so I think she'll hold together.

Those parachute jumps I told you about came off this afternoon. Sure glad I got to see them. They used a big Ford ship, has three motors. Same as Floyd Bennett's and the one Mrs. Lindbergh flew to Mexico in. They broke the Navy's parachute jump record. We all missed supper to see them. It was the prettiest thing I ever saw. They all dived out of that door one after the other. The chutes opened perfectly and there they were, all ten of them, strung out parallel to the rows of hangars. They all landed safely and at practically the same time. They cleared that ship in 8 and 1/5 seconds! Sure was something, you may see pictures. They had a newsreel man alongside in a DH, one on top of a hangar, and a third movie camera was strapped to the side of the fuselage about 10 feet ahead of the door.

Orv

4th Composite Group, Air Corps
Camp Nichols
Rizal, Philippine Islands
May 20 - 28

Folks,

Our bunch arrived in great shape. We passed in by the old walled city. The Spaniards built a wall around old Manila, you know. It's fairly high & is of

14

Orvis took a number of pictures of the record jump at Chanute. Parachuting was still considered the work of real daredevils.

stone. Still mounted with cannon.

We passed Corregidor when we went through the straits. That's the island fortress that guards the entrance to the bay. I understand it is the heaviest fortified place in the world.

Manila Harbor is protected by a long breakwater and has been dredged out. One of the ships in port is a German cruiser, the "Berlin." It's a cadet training ship for the German Navy.

Traffic is all left handed and most of the cars have the wheel on the right side. Are a lot of "one hoss shays." Horses are hardly larger than ponies. All houses are thatched, really nothing but shacks.

We are about a ten minute walk from the beach but haven't been down there yet. I got so terribly sunburned surfing off Waikiki Beach in Hawaii that I am not in any hurry to have a renewed encounter with Mr. Sun. I understand there are quite a few sharks around.

Camp Nichols is five or six miles from the heart of Manila. Can go in on a street car for about sixteen cents. Have a different money system over here, Pesos and Centavos. One Peso equals fifty cents.

Orv

P.S. We start right off photo-mapping the coastline tomorrow, which I understand will be our primary job - to aid in the defense of the Philippines.

Lansing, Mich.
May 29, 1928

Myrtle,

Hello cheri, how are you? Got your very welcome letter and cake today. Do you know cheri, I'd rather get a letter from you than any other three people I know.

You know why? Because I believe you're the most interesting girl I ever met. No I was not swearing at you in French in my last letter - the closest I'll probably ever come will be to call you "dearest sweetheart, m'love" or something like that, providing of course, I would be considered worthy of such an honor. I'm serious you see cheri, I've grown quite attached to you. But anon for that.

15

U.S.A.T. Chateau Thierry.

Manila Harbor and a portion of the U.S. Pacific Fleet in 1928.
All these four-pipe destroyers have canvass rigged up on the decks to protect
the men from the brutal tropical sun – in this the days before air conditioning.

Say, I have only seen a photo of your log cabin but I'm in love with it already. I can see it nestled among the whispering trees, while not far away the placid lake gathers and reflects the rays from a beautiful summer moon. I can hear the screech of the owl in the distance as it's plaintive note drifts down to me across the still waters. I can hear the moan of the wind as it sighs among the green limbs of the beautiful pines, and the answering note of the evening song of the birds as they prepare for their rest. I can see a chair for two drawn up before the fireplace, and the dancing flames casting their shadows in grotesque shapes on the rustic walls. It seems to me that God would have such a place for a little nest for two, doesn't it to you?

I love nature. I love the woods, the laughing

brooks, the placid streams. It seems the wooded hilltops and meadowed valleys are a part of me. Often I dream of such a place where I long to be with the one whom God has made and chosen for me. To such a place would I like to fly, leaving behind the cares and strifes of the world. A place to work, a place to play, and a place where one could stand with arms uplifted to the starry heavens above and say deep in his heart, as David did, "The cattle on a thousand hills are thine, O Lord . . . In thee will I find my joy and my happiness."

With my love, Ted
Theodore R. Jones

The Breeze Hill log cabin Ted is swooning over.
The fact that this stone chimney, built in 1924, is still in terrific condition
at the time of the millenium is a testament to Mamie's building ability.

Camp Nichols airfield. There are no hard surface runways, only large sod strips parallel to the prevailing winds.

The Aitkin Republican

A J Anderson 23527

LARGEST CIRCULATION
MOST COMPLETE NEWS

The Official and Leading Newspaper of Aitkin County

AITKIN, AITKIN COUNTY, MINNESOTA, THURSDAY, JUNE 14, 1928.

SUBSCRIPTION $1.50 A YEAR

Hoover Nomination Expected To Take Place Today

Flower Bedecked Lawns Help Make Aitkin One of Most Attractive Places in State

**SHOW SPECIAL INTER-
YEAR WITH IMPROVE-
TEST IN PROGRESS**

...utiful, well-kept
...lots of paint, in-
...ise of flowers
...for decora-

**Community Picnic
Next Wednesday**

The committee in charge of the Community Picnic, officially set for Wednesday next, met last evening to formulate plans. The speaker for the occasion has not as yet been definitely ...m Bureau, will not F. Reed, president of the The Republican re-...nent from state head-...ne ago that he had ...June 16th. Later ...red this date, im-

...the fair grounds
...ails; otherwise
...ry. There will
...Melody Jacks,
...o five, and a
...ing in con-
...ning Satur-
...auspices.
...promised
...lock.

DAWES, HOUGHTON, McNIDER BOOMED AS RUNNING MATES

**TEST VOTE ASSURES THAT COM-
MERCE SECRETARY WILL BE G.
O. P. STANDARD BEARER**

Herbert Hoover will be nominated as Republican candidate for the presidency of the United States, it is definitely assured, in official balloting to take place at the convention in Kansas City today. In a convention roll call taken yesterday the approximate division of Hoover and anti-Hoover strength was quite clearly revealed. In the showdown Secretary of the Treasury Mellon cast all of Pennsylvania's 79 votes for the Hoover-Creager slate, which also got all of the votes from Massachusetts, including that of Chairman Butler of the national committee, and 31 of the 90 from New York state, which is opposed to the Great Lakes-St. Lawrence Waterway proposals, which Hoover definitely favors. The final result was 676½ votes for the Hoover nomination, and 359½ against, with a small contingent of the convention delegates absent or barred because of technicalities.

Vicepresident Charles G. Dawes and ...nson B. Houghton, ambassador to ...rmany immediately following the ..., are most likely at present among th? possible running mates. Iowa is ...ealing strongly for Hanford Mc-N...or, former national chief of the A...erican Legion.

...or the first time in the history of ...a country a president has continued ... nomination, even

Orvis Nelson Will Relate Adventure of His Pacific Trip in Travelogue Series

CLIFFORD L. HILTON

**POPULAR TAMARACK YOUTH
SERVING WITH AVIATION CORPS
ASSIGNED TO INTERESTING
DUTY**

The Republican will publish a travelogue beginning with this issue, which will be written from time to time by Orvis Nelson, son of Mr. and Mrs. Marcus Nelson of Tamarack and Minneapolis. Orvis is aboard the U. S. A. T., "Chateau Thierry," in Carribean waters. The first letter received is dated Friday, May 18th. On the Tuesday following, the ship docked at Cristobal, Panama.

Mr. Nelson arrived on the west coast June 2nd, and was sent to Ft. McDowell, California, on Friday. He set sail again in Pacific waters on the U. S. Grant. Honolulu will be the first stop. Guam next.

Orvis is a popular youth and his letter is written in a highly interesting vein. The Republican is certain that his many friends and others will look forward to publication of this series. He is assigned to do photography in the Hawaiian Island, the Philippines, and various other places from airships, as he is enlisted with an aviation unit. The pictures thus taken will be fitted together as mosaics forming maps which will be reproduced by the United States government, thus serving as very valuable geographical data. Orvis received his aviation training in Illinois.

Friday May 18, 1928,
12:30 p. m.

At sea on the U. S. A. T.
"Chateau Thierry".

We were up early Wednesday morning and soon had breakfast and what police work we had to do out of the way. We got all our bags together and carried them down to the south end of the Parade Ground, near the dock. Here we lined up in the companies as they were organized the day before. I am in the first section of the

**JUDGE HILTON IS
LOGICAL NOMINEE**

Among the nominations to be made at the primary election is one for justice of the supreme court, and one of the candidates for this nomination is ... Clifford L. Hilton. He is so ... own throughout the state that ...s hardly any doubt about his ... chosen next Monday. For many ...he was the attorney general of ...tate and so well did Governor ...rianson think of his ability as a ...er and his peculiar fitness for ...e that when a vacancy occurred ...e supreme court the first of January last he appointed Mr. Hilton to attain-Ameri-body a presi-...eman.

On the car Indypls
June 28, 1928

Mom & Dad,

Orv sent clippings from the Manila papers with those pictures & article. He has been sending in articles about his experiences to the Aitkin Republican too. And Aunt Dilla got a $15 check from the Indianapolis Star, which I'll put in the bank for him. 'Member how he used to talk about getting his name in the paper?

Here is a copy of his latest piece in the Aitkin Republican. Isn't it splendidly written? Orv can make you see, feel, or hear just what he wishes. If I could write like him, I'd flood magazine offices with articles.

Everyone is dash here - dash there. Whoops! We're here. Another Monday morning & it's back to work.

Myrtle

Hula Dancer, Hawaiian Islands.

HONOLULU

*Miniature pennant and postcard
Orvis bought in Honolulu*

18

Indypls
Sat. Sept 29, 1928

Mom and Dad,

The idea of a new floor and other improvements at the cabin sounds nice, Mom, but don't over do. You try to do so much.

Hap's stomach has been off so we haven't tried the fruit cake yet. He was so tickled about it.

Dad, I know there is a rough class of girls in a good many places, but one just has to ignore the vulgarity and act and talk as one should. It is all much easier for me than it would be for a younger girl. You'd be surprised at the number of divorces I've come in contact with. Many of them are rather hard boiled specimens.

If I keep trying to tune this radio perhaps I'll be good at it in about a hundred years. So far I'm best at getting squawks and squeaks.

Myrtle

Mamie and Scottie.

```
                          NO DOG

     No muddy dog tracks on the floor; our food contains no hair; no
 marks on windows any more where cold nose rested there; no nest made
 on forbidden bed; no dog to walk in rain; no urgent pleading to be
 fed; no sweeping hairs in vain.

     When doorbell rings, no fearsome growls; no nips at callers' legs;
 fire siren starts no lonely howls; at mealtimes, no one begs; no barks
 at rabbits in the wood; we're free to go away a day or week if in the
 mood--no kennel bill to pay.

     No sleeping dog by fireplace curled; when we come in, no fuss;
 No eyes to say in all the world he loves no one but us;
 No wagging tail; no head on knee;  no guard when darkness thickens;
 no eager plea for romp or spree; We miss him like the dickens.
```

Myrtle's requiem to Hector, another longtime family dog.

Indypls
Oct 12, 1928

Dad,

Thx load for the five spot but I feel guilty taking it as I know how hard cash is to come by.

I think Indiana will go for Hoover, but elect a democratic governor. Leslie, the Republican candidate, is like Al Smith - talks too much. And he doesn't stick to the truth only about 5 times out of 10.

What are you going to do with Mother this winter? Tamarack is no place for her as it is too unhealthy. She'd be sick all year. And she won't be able to stay at the lake all that much longer.

Thanks for the offer to work at the store but Tamarack is about as dead a place as there is. I'll stick here for now.

Myrtle

Sandy Lake
Oct 16-28

Darling Myrtle,

I am fixing up the kitchen in my cabin. Had a time getting up the steam, got only about 1/3 done as have to move things alone. Got tired and stopped earlier than usual today.

I have to cut off the door too - will not close right. Have some moulding to make a better fit. Has gate hinges so will not be easy.

My new pup Scottie wants to go out and chase chipmunks but I feel like sitting. When I went after the mail to Anderson's he lit out across the bridge like a team of horses, so much noise. I miss old Heck like "heck."

I have not been over to Aitkin for some time as Dad has been doing the going. He did not come back so suppose he went on to Gull. He got rare chuckle out of Tingdale other day when he told him "that country over to Brainerd has such fine lakes the water runs all the way up to the shore."

I am burning some pine brush. Makes a flashy fire. I keep a fire most of time.

Am not looking forward to moving to T-K. I sure dislike that gossipy place, but guess will have to see what Dad says, maybe we can got to Mpls.

Mom

P.S. Dad been unloading coal, sure bad for his lungs.

Hunting around Sandy Lake

When it came time for serious hunting & fishing, you looked to (left to right) Ernest Nelson, Maurice Nelson and Haakon Friestad.

Mamie was always comfortable around firearms. During the pony farm years, she kept a pump action .22 rifle handy to drive away garden pests and the like. Here she is duck hunting with Maurice Nelson.

This big bear appeared in several postcards & promotional efforts.

When the hunting slowed, the boys turned to pranks. This little scene is happening near the Prairie River mouth. Those two fellows look uncomfortably close to deep, open water but it's actually the shoreline.

Sandy Lake
Oct 18-28

Darling Myrtle,
Finished the floor of the kitchen today and boy it's really cute now. I want to put a window in as it's too dark to cook. I have the ice box & stove back in - new cupboard up. Built a woodbox and put in some nails for kettles and pans.

Marcus sent up some Mpls. duck hunters to the shack he threw up next door. Guess he got a little out of them. I told them help yourself to the wood pile & pump. They took their boat and stuff and are camping on the island beyond Battle Island. They call it Goat Island that is a new one on me (Moose Gut Dad says it is).

I caught 3 mice last nite. I got to trap ever nite now to get rid of them, they know winter is coming.
Mom

Sandy Lake
Oct 20-28

Girlie,
They are talking of snow but it's really very mild. Cabin looks just wonderful now, like a real home. Will get that window in kitchen if I can get a hole started. Have to work on Dad I guess.

Dad gave J.P. Brenner a good call down today in T-K for working for Al Smith for President. He had him hedging.

The boys froze out on the island. Only got 4 ducks, are hundreds but they stay in middle of the lake and rise up high when they take off.

I'd like to go to church tomorrow but if Dad don't come I can't. I just have gas enough for one trip and I have to go for supplys soon.

I will cook some prunes and apple sauce and some bean soup. Better come over for dinner. ha. I have finally gotten your Father to eat sweet potatoes, he asks for them now.

Went up hill to garden & dug out a last few onions, potatoes, picked 3 quarts of raspberries. Not much account. Still a lot of clover in the little clearing. Air smells so crisp and the sun seems brighter this time of year than any other. Leaves all over but they will have to stay there. Has been a great Fall. I sure feel good now. Last nite was a good sleeping nite.

This morning Dad wanted to know my plans for Mpls. I said I just wanted one or two furnished rooms so I could cook a little. I thot be best in N. part of town some place air is better and is cheaper rent.
Mom

Sandy Lake
Oct 27-28

Girlie,
Have the brush work done on the floor and am over the varnish fever as Carr used to call my paint spells.

Dad brought home some beefsteak last eve., so we had it, gravy, and sweet potatoes. Best steak we had in ages. He & Paul been cooking up a scheme - plan to open a series of chain stores, sell for cash. Geo. Steffer is to run one at McGregor. The wholesalers at Duluth are to back it. If it goes good at McGregor they will spread out all along the two railroads. Is to be Nelson-Heller Co. but I think Wheeler is going in it too. If it's a success Dad will get a salary be head of it with Paul to check up and do detail. Paul & Geo. are all excited. Wheeler wanted to fire Paul because he had been fussy at me but Paul will be O.K. now for Dad gave him a good call down.

Dad likes to eat in kitchen. We use my little table, I put my white & yellow cloth on every evening. He will be done at Gull in a few days. I heard was taking more money than they expected. Built too fine, I thot so all along.
Mom

Sandy Lake
Oct 30-28

Darling Myrtle,
Got back from Tamarack late as had a blow out. One of wheels I mean tires Marcus got last Fall. Went way of all flesh. I see George forgot to put in butter for me.

Took me forever in town on account I worked so long scrubbing the chicken manure off the dining room table. Was taken into that small shed and when Paul put chickens in the chump left the furniture in there and was a sight.

I got me new slippers also goods for to make me a "com own a." It's not pretty but is warm, heavy and fleese. Is it an S or a Z on fleece. Guess it's a C. Ha. Ha.

I have a very large fire as house got cold during my absence.

Brenner was talking up Smith again at bank. I can't see why he wants him in, most of them want to be ruled by the Pope in Rome.
Mom

Indypls
Tues a.m. Nov 6, 1928

Folks,

Much excitement about the election. Everybody in the house has taken turns explaining the voting machines to Laura and at that, I'll bet she makes a mistake.

Was out with Hap Sat. nite. He has been wearing a Smith pin all the time & I never did notice it until then. He got a huge kick out of having me worried.

Finally got a letter from Orv. Been so long. He's O.K. but I guess the boats are irregular now because of storms. He wants so much when he comes home to go back to college & get a degree. The Army flying schools now require a degree for entrance. Did he write that he has been taking pilot lessons?

Myrtle

P.S. Orv sent a poem one of the guys, O'Connor, wrote. Kind of nice, eh?

```
They have a guy in the photo section,
Nelson is his name/
  No matterwhere you see him,
  He alway is the  same,

He knows twice as much a s  the best of them,
And his sperits never sag,
He does his work as he sees fit,
and you never hear him brag,

When it comes to playing football,
  That fellow sure is neat,
  He plays a game at center xxxxx
  That sure is hard to beat,


You always see him with a smile,
From beginning of day to the end,
And I know it is worth a kings ransom,
To have Nelson call you his friend/

                    Buster O'Connor
                    The Jewish short timer/
```

Indypls
Nov 13, '28

Mom & Dad,

Aunt Dilla is ironing now after she washed my clothes in her new Apex Washer (Electric). Does washing with much less labor - has spinners instead of wringers & they are almost dry enough to iron when they come out.

Aunt Dilla has had me up on my ear the last two days kidding me about smoking. She kept saying that she heard I smoked & I wondered who the dickens had such a pipe dream. I said well somebody was crazy. And she just ha haed. She had been trying to get my goat. They all tease the gizzard out of me.

Myrtle

Sandy Lake
Nov 14-28

Myrtle,

Dad got home from Mpls the other day, was supposed to be back sooner but I suppose he remembered Armistice Day and staid. You know he has to take in everything or thinks he has to.

Dad and Wheeler trying to fix up about stores. They expect to be here soon.

I will send Big Boy letters on. His football coach told him he was 1/3 of team in the game with the

Orvis (playing center) and the Camp Nichols football team.

22

submarine boys. Nichols beat them 21 to 0. He has been very busy with his aerial mapping and photographing important doings. He has sent us hundreds of pictures. Dad is wild over them. I hope he can go some place to a university, need to be a college graduate to be president. ha. ha.

We are to move to Tamarack tomorrow. Dad could not get a place in Mpls for now. I will be busy closing up out here. Carr will haul things down.

Mom

P.S. It snowed last nite and it's so cold damp that it penetrates.

Tamarack, Minn.
Nov 20-28

Josie Tingdale
    C/O Tingdale Bros., Mpls
Sister-in-law,

Marcus decided we can not come down to Mpls, am moved to Tamarack to a place in the middle of a field a mile from town. We sure feel blue to think we lost that chance on the flat. We also lost others as we have been trying all Fall to get a place. Perhaps you will hear of something we can get, I enclose our references that can be given out.

I never lived in such a small house. It hurts to see the old place so close, we ourselves were well fixed until we got burned out and Tamarack Forest Products Co. failed. I don't want to stay here & can not stand carrying water so far either. I have about 32 hens & get 20 eggs some days but I have trouble getting them to town.

If you find anything for us down there for what we can pay let us know soons you can.

As ever, Mamie N.

Tamarack
Nov 22-28

Myrtle,

I had planned to call on Mrs. Douglas today but too windy. I will bake her a pumpkin pie tomorrow.

I heard that P.'s new wife is a Catholic. Can you beat it? Carr says she was considered a "fast" one at Lawler. Dad says she looks like Barney Google.

I've lost three lbs. since I came to T-K. I will try to gain again. I bought two apples and they are sure busters. Got some dates too but they are too sweet.

Orvis sent a picture of one of his officers with

Orvis with a suitably clothed Filipino woman. She is holding a cigarette in her left hand, while balancing Orvis' umbrella in her head basket.

his hands on the breast of two savage women. Dad was horrified and wanted to send for him at once but I had my suspicions he was playing a trick on me for I knew he had not been on that Island himself. I wrote him I thot his officer was a nasty man. In todays letter he said he did it for fun to get a rise out of me. Said those women just fill him with disgust and nausea. Of course, they are savages and know no better. He sent along another batch of naked women with just a tee string, Kid has them all named for my benefit. I know he did not take them. I can hear him sniggering.

Mom

P.S. I suppose I sound kiddish about living at T-K but I had so many lonely and sick years here I feel as if I'd go wild to live here all the time. I told Dad to get to work on going to Mpls.

Tamarack
Dec 1-28

Myrtle,

Mrs. Douglas & Mayhall came last nite to see Orvis' pictures and as it takes from 2 to 3 hrs. to see properly we were late getting to bed. Dad went anyway.

Yesterday I washed. They fixed the well so we think it may do but it's still muddy tho.

I guess Paul won't go along with the chain store. He is afraid. Dad may have to give up on the idea.

Carr and Dad are like two little boys running around and fixing things. Fixed steps today and now are gone to try some "detective" work to see who stole the cow stanchions from out of Kelley's barn. They started to Duluth the other day and got to the county line and froze the engine. Then it got so hot it caught fire in the part that is covered over where oil pan is. Cracked cylinder head and split valves so Dad had to send off for it to be fixed. He hated to buy alcohol when he was going to return it to Paul today but it was fatal economy.

Mom

Tamarack
Dec 3-28

Myrtle,

Dad is going to Duluth to Hughes trial tomorrow. He gets a kick out of trials as you know. I will stay with Mrs. Mayhall tonite and Doc. Snader tomorrow, if Dad stays that long. I shan't give Mother Heller and Mrs. Mayhall any opportunity to talk about me.

Carr went to s.s. and church with me yesterday. The other day we had quite a discussion on the Bible & found we agreed on some things and on some we do not. Knows his Bible pretty well. He looked fine, like a dignified old man. I pressed his suit, Dad shined his shoes, and we gave him Dad's old overcoat and a cap too small for him. You be surprised how nice he looked and he enjoyed it too.

Myrtle and Mamie looking at a photo Orvis took out in the Philippine bush.

24

He has promised me to go this year. It may have some effect on Dad.

After church, I hurried away to dinner with Mrs. Douglas. She was worried for fear I'd back out and met me like a long lost child. I do not want to let them get such a hold on me for I do not like to account for everplace I go to the neighbors.

I came home at 3 and Dad was asleep and Carr reading. I got after Dad for not writing Orvis in time for Christmas so he wrote him & you today but Orvis won't get it till after Christmas now.

Dad aims to sell lots on Sandy for Marshall-Wells this winter. He kind of surprised me when he said he'd always dreamed of being a lawyer but knew he never could for want of education. He would have been good at it.

Mom

P.S. Some say was 10 below last nite some 19 some 14 old DiDi Martin says 20 so there you are can take your choice.

NELSON & HELLER CO.
TAMARACK, MINN.

Dec. 3/28

Daughter,

Will write a few lines as snow is so deep I can't do any hiking around. We are living nicely near town but are planning on going to Mpls before long.

I think your Mother is feeling pretty well. She says she thinks she is getting fat. I suppose it's my cooking as I am sure a good cook.

Carr is happy as a sun shower sawing wood and shoveling snow. We are getting ready to ship a car of scrap iron so he and I have been busy for the last few days packing up junk.

Business in the store is picking up some. I am going to Duluth tomorrow Hughes Lawsuit take a day I guess. Going by train as snow too deep to drive, unless the snow plow goes through today. The bread truck just came with reports of bad road & lots of cars stalled.

They had quite a feed here Thanksgiving Day but not like your Mother used to make. I hope she don't forget how to roast a turkey - does the best I ever ate.

Your Mother had dinner with Mrs. Douglas at the Newby Hotel. Carr and I had a feast at the house. Had a fine roast and all that goes with it. I slept all afternoon after eating.

Guess will quit for this time.

Dad

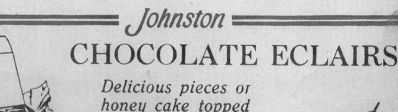

Camp Nichols, P.I.
Dec 10, 1928

Folks,

Went on a cross country last week, went up on maneuvers. First time in history here that a Pvt. went on maneuvers from the Section. Always non-coms before. I flew in one of the Army's latest planes, the Douglas ORH Bluebird. Lot of darkroom work when we landed.

Maybe you think holding that fifty pounds of camera out in the slip stream isn't work. My legs ache for three days from bracing myself. I stand up for practically a whole hour, then sit down long enough to get my wind and rest my arms while the Lieut. circles around into position again.

Are you wondering what I did with the pigeons? There were eight altogether, and I turned them loose when we reached Clark Field. They circled around for quite awhile before heading back to Nichols. They take

The photographer is in the rear seat. His camera looks like the barrel of a cannon.

the pigeons out for practice like that every few days.

Tell Myrtle she should try to get her money back on the customs duty. All soldiers gifts are duty free; they should not have collected on it at all. Let me know if I need to write to someone.

Orv

P.S. Got word I am promoted to Second Class Air Mechanic. Fancy title to do the same job but will be for more money.

G. Sommers & Co.
Saint Paul, Minn.
December 11, 1928

Nelson Heller Co.
    Tamarack, Minn.
Gentlemen:

On August 15, 1928, Herbert Hoover's Department of Commerce issued a bulletin titled "Independent Merchants" which contained these sentences: "SOME OBSERVERS PREDICT THE ELIMINATION OF THE INDEPENDENT MERCHANT.

Orvis and his aerial camera.

26

THE DEPARTMENT OF COMMERCE HOLDS NO SUCH BELIEF."

This company is willing to go on record that we are prepared to fight to a finish for the independent merchant. He must, and will, be protected and allowed to grow and prosper.

We do not operate retail stores or chain stores; we are not in mergers and we do not expect to sell out to anyone. We make these emphatic statements to contradict the rumors that are spread abroad.

It is true that a large wholesale firm in a neighboring city has just announced that they are about to operate a chain of retail variety and department stores throughout this section. Our own attitude is unchanged. Our friends are the independent retail merchants and we shall back them to the limit in their fight with this new and unexpected competition.

We are now working on a new plan for helping the independent merchant to fight the Chains. As soon as we are ready you will hear from us. Meanwhile, I shall be glad to have you tell me what you think of the subject discussed in this letter.

B. Sommers, Prest.

ALL PRICES, AGREEMENTS AND CONTRACTS ARE MADE CONTINGENT UPON STRIKES, ACCIDENTS, DELAYS TO CARRIERS AND OTHER DELAYS, UNAVOIDABLE OR BEYOND OUR CONTROL, OR BY FIRE.

TAMARACK FOREST PRODUCTS CO.
PRODUCERS AND WHOLESALERS
POSTS, POLES, PILING, TIES, PULPWOOD AND LOGS
LUMBER

YARD AND MILL:
TAMARACK, MINN.

TAMARACK, MINN.   December, 12th./28.

B. Sommers Pres.
G. Sommers & Co.
          St. Paul, Minn.
Dear Sir.

We are in receipt of yours of the 11th. regarding the Chain Retail Stores of one of the Now Whole Sale Houses, we had noticed the the News Item, as per inclosed Clipping.

There must be some effort made by the Independent Dealers to survive, the change in the trend of Business, just what that will be is a big problem.
We feel that the independent merchant, must get the benefit of larger buying power, cut out credits, take advantage of discounts, and in every way reduce overhead, inorder to compete with the chain stores.

With such houses as Butler Bros. going into the retail business, will I suppose drive others into the smaller towns, and in this way effect all Independent Merchants both large and small, and will unless stoped, drive the independents out of business.

The average small Merchant can stay in the game by selling for cash, and not let the Credit business clean him out as there is nnnnnn but what most failures are due to Credits with Poor collections, and the ambition to do a Volum business instead of being satisfied, with such business as will be cash. The chain store gets the cash, and has no particular interest in the development of the comunity, as they change managers, and help so often that they do become a part of the comunity, they live in, but are there just to get the business, which of course is a good idea, for them but not best for the comunity.

We will be very glad to hear from you again regarding this matter as soon as your plans are completed, as we are surely interested in it and hope to be able to stay in the game.

          Yours very truly.
          NELSON HELLER COMPANY.
          By _____ Pres.

Marcus' first draft response to Mr. Sommers' letter.

Tamarack
December 12th, 1928

Hello Orvis,

I answered your letter last week but Mae found it and read it, and I was so angry that I threw the letter in the stove. Too bad too, for it was quite a letter.

Today the wedding bells ring out. Louise is to be married - I hate to remind you of it because I know just how you feel but you will have to be told the sad truth sooner or later. I wasn't invited - I guess I'm too small potatoes for her. They say she has quite a cute outfit and Kai said she was going up early to see to it that her stockings were on straight and her under skirt didn't show. It's a good thing she's going to be safely married. We girls call her a public menace, she vamps all our boy friends.

I suppose you heard about the new Farmer's Store they have in Chas. MacDonald's building. The Lawler Farmer's Cooperative Association is running the place. They opened Monday - will carry Gen. Merch., Dry Goods, and Farm Machinery. I guess they will try to run all the other

Merry Christmas from [Alice] Manila P.I. 1928

1831 Park Ave. Mpls
Jan 9th, 1929

Girlie,

We are settling in to yet another place. I'm beginning to feel like a gypsy. I went out job hunting and I made a good impression at Stowel Art Studio. She said my work was good and would put me to work but now for a while have very little to do but for me to be sure and come back later and believe me I expect to. I want to keep going to Art School. I still have ambition to amount to something and am almost 50. Just so money holds out.

Dad has a lot of deals on and sure makes me glad. Now Tingdale wants him back but I tell him and he feels same be better work independent - good deals go to them and he gets the penny stuff.

This is a four flat bldg. Not new but not old either. Is quiet but not so warm. You ought to see me sit up high on the radiator.

Mom

stores in town out of business. I expect your Dad & Paul are none to happy.

DARN BOLSHEVIKS! That's all they are. It is a Finlander outfit and not even decent Finns. Nick Louma says they are a disgrace to Finn Land. Unless you join their "I Want Work" organization you can't work in their stores. They won't recognize the American flag and they claim they aren't raising their young men to fight for America.

As Ever, Vivian Cyrus

Tamarack
Dec 28-28

Darling Myrtle,

Dad says we will go to Mpls after all so I will be busy getting everything ready. He is asleep tho only a little after six. He sleeps so much I'd like to get him examined.

For supper we had French fried bread and turkey hash and nice mealy potatoes. The cheesing made the hash good.

Mom

Mpls
Jan 12-29

Girlie,

Well, I was over to the Clinic all day yesterday and believe me I was tired last nite. I have been passing blood in my bowels. They want to rush me right over to University Hospital but I wanted to wait till Dad came as I did not have enough money. Cost $7.00 for operating room and $3.00 per day for bed unless I wanted the expense put on County and I, of course, do not consider myself a Co. charge. It seems is a chance I have cancer or what will cause cancer. Of course, I should have had a chest exam every 6 months as they have always advised me to but while I knew I was not well seemed like I never got to go see about it. Now don't worry sis it may not amount to anything as they will EXray me first and will not operate unless must do so. I go back Monday. Dr. advised me again to start a budget in our family but if it ever got clear around it'd take about 5 years. ha. ha.

Mom

Tamarack
Jan 20/1929

Daughter,

Your Mother got thro operation in fine shape. Gave her Gas so she was not so sick afterwards. Was not as serious as could have been, so she feels better now that it is over. Has good color, not eating anything yet but soft food.

We hope she will be up and around in a couple of weeks so lets not worry. I will get a nice warm apt for her so she will be able to get along without worry.

I will go back to Mpls in the morning and try to see her tomorrow nite. Visiting hours are at wrong time of day for a working man.

Dad

Camp Nichols, P.I.
Sunday, Jan 20th, 1929

Folks,

Thanks for sending on my latest article to the Aitkin Republican. I sent some photographs to the National Geographic but I don't suppose they'll use them.

We've laid around last four days, reading, sleeping, & coloring a few pictures. Go back to work on the old schedule tomorrow so we have to get up at 5:30 again instead of when we felt like. We only stand reveille when Lt. Goddard is Officer of the Day to make him think we stand it all the time. Believe me, we have it soft. One forgets he's in the Army - almost.

Goddard pulled me aside and told me I am to be promoted to Sergeant without Air Mechanic Rating. The exam was just duck-soup for me. In other words, I've gotten all the breaks. Been here six months and get the best rating in the Section - for Private that is. Pays $72 gold so it's better than "Buck" Sergeant, which only pays $54. There are going to be lots of fellows howling when they find out. Well, ish kabibble. It's every dog for himself. They all had more than an equal chance.

So long, Orv

Camp Nichols, P.I.
February 5th 1929

Myrtle,

Everyone has been writing & asking when I'll return to the Good Old U.S.A. Beats me. Let me know what you think. I mean about Mom & Dad's health. If they are getting along O.K. I haven't gotten any mail from them for nearly 3 weeks. I might stay another year but if they'd be better off for my being in the states, I'd better go back. Slip me a hint. I will either go to college here part-time or there full-time this fall.

We're practicing football a half hour every afternoon. Play next Sunday down at the Carnival.

Orv

4009 Nokomis Ave So. Mpls
Feb 9-29

Darling Myrtle,

We rented a wonderful new apartment, big corner room with a bathroom and kitchenette with a real gas stove. Murphy bed and a day bed. The kitchen is what is called a Pullman - big doors shut if off. $10.50 a week and we have to pay for gas and electric lights. I thot high but he wants a bath so can't get much less. It has cost a good deal to eat out and I don't care for it either so will try to cook here. I need to take extra food to build up my blood.

I just had a cup of cocoa. I got used to it got babyed at the hospital so some of others said but it was because I needed to be kept on my back due to the wounds on my chest. We paid cash, too. None of rest did, but that cuts no ice there as very few pay even tho they can do so.

I forgot to have Dad get me more writing paper and had to use this piece of brown sack. I am not able to walk far to get some & he always forgets. I must get after him to bring me some.

I would advise for enlarged pores to wash face in cold plain water in morning. Use warm water & soap at nite, rinse off, then cold. Orvis & I always use lots of cold water and our pores are not so bad.

Dad wants you to write C/O his office for now.

Mom

P.S. Dad opens all my letters that come to office. I bet he'd roar if I opened his. Fixed salt pork in beans last nite and he sure loved it. Was all the meat I had in the house.

Camp Nichols, P.I.
Feb 22, 1929

Mom,

The latest mail brought me distressing and then reassuring news that the operation was over and as I haven't received any cables I'm sure you got out O.K. Last I heard you were going in for a check up so was quite a shock. Hope your health will be better from now on. Well, if you could be here today you could take a sun bath. Hot! And how!

Did you every hear the tune "Dixie Vagabond?" I bought the record a week ago. Is sung by the Rounders.

Had some real excitement a while back. We went out to photograph the Grant coming in and time was hanging heavy on my hands next day so I proceeded to make a composite photo of an O-2H flying upside down alongside the deck of the ship. The picture came out beautifully and it was almost impossible to tell it was a fake. The photo was an instant success and made the rounds at the Army and Navy Club and the Manila Hotel. Douglas MacArthur, Commanding General of the Philippine Department, got hold of a copy and became highly incensed that one of his pilots would pull such a stunt. It was some time before the General was persuaded it was all a joke. I was afraid I might be in dutch but haven't heard anything more about it so guess it's O.K. Later, I made a friend of a planter here and he got me into a society affair and both MacArthur and Henry Stimson, Governor General of the P.I., were in attendance. I got to meet both of them (I had on my new white suit & made up I was a civilian businessman!) and believe me they are a couple of powerful characters. So you see, I am getting around a little for a lowly enlisted man.

Orv

The famous fake photograph. Orvis did a pretty good job; no wonder General MacArthur was fooled!

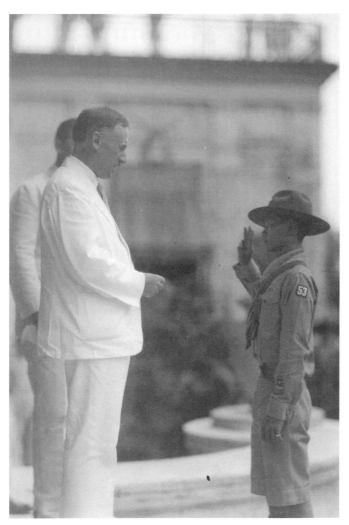

Governor General Stimson meets a Filipino Boy Scout.

THE YOUTH'S COMPANION
BOSTON, MASSACHUSETTS

We regret that we are compelled to decline the manuscript you have kindly submitted to us for examination.

For various reasons a manuscript may not be adapted to The Youth's Companion and yet may meet with acceptance elsewhere. The return of a manuscript, therefore, does not necessarily imply lack of merit or unfitness for publication.

We consider it a favor to be allowed to examine manuscripts, whether they prove acceptable or not.

Please excuse the absence of specific criticism, which is rendered impossible by the great number of manuscripts submitted to us.

Thanking you for your courtesy, we are,

Very truly yours,

The Editors

Myrtle worked particularily hard at her writing during the Rockwood Pulley days. Unfortunately, she was never published. This is a form rejection letter (they haven't changed much) she received postmarked Feb 28, 1929.

Mpls
Mar 5-29

Girlie,

You'd laugh if you had been here Sat. nite. Dad said he not be back till late so when I was getting a stamp (are scarce as hen's teeth here) on way back about 2 blocks away is a movie - 10 cent comic pictures. Well, I felt like do me some good so went in and staid till about 11 and in meantime Dad came home. He had no key and because I had left lights on he thought I was sick or worse and was the reason I did not answer. So he got a key of janitor and got in and saw I was gone. Then he got kind of mad I guess, cause he had been scared and so, of course, I got a little calling down when I came. I wanted to laugh but did not dare. He will have a key from now on.

I moped around the house all day today. They burn soft coal here and if it goes in our lungs like it does on floors and everything else, it is none to healthy, but Dad wants to stick around close to down town. He is bleeding at nose a good deal again. He's got to do something for his high blood pressure.

About feeling so run down better get you some Hagee's Cod Liver oil. The fishy part is out so it is not bad at all to take but costs some more. Do not get any other but Hagee's or the pure oil for rest are bad on heart & not safe to take.

Mom

P.S. Got a long letter from Big Boy. Dad is proud of Orvis tho he tries not to show it. He teases the life out of me when he gets a spell. I don't mean he is not proud of his girl too Myrtle.

Mpls
March 23-29

Myrtle,

Orvis wrote he has decided he wants to buy his way out of Army in April or May. We not sure if Dad can get the $170 by that time or not, $120 to buy out and $50 more for overseas discharge. Orvis wants us to smell out a job of aerial survey work for summer, then go to college next fall.

Mom

Indypls
March 28, '29

Dad & Mom,

After you read the enclosed wedding notice, send it on to Orv. Old G.A. Rockwood has gone to Europe for the wedding, if it ever takes place. I guess he's pretty sore about it, and the girl isn't very crazy about the prince either, but her mother is determined. I guess G.A. thinks it'll be another one to support. The fellow can't even get a passport into the U.S. except for short visits. They'll have to live abroad.

Work same as usual. Pulleys, pulleys, pulleys. The old bachelor shipping clerk - age about 40 - takes me to town every night from Rockwood's. Makes it possible to get home at least 15 minutes sooner. Surely is good to me. Poor old bird has lost all his folks, lives in a bachelor apartment, and I guess he likes to have someone to blow off steam to.

I've been too tired nights to go out much. Johnny Hamilton, Hiram, & I are the "home gang." At first I used to get dates for both girl cousins, but I guess they've forgotten that. I've quit doing it and I won't go with the kids alone so I just don't go.

Myrtle

P.S. Every place in town, but at Rockwood's I think, is off from 12 to 3 for Good Friday church tomorrow. Wish we could. There are signs up all over - "He gave His life - give Him three hours."

Indypls
April 2, 1929

Dad & Mom,

On All Fools Day we called Aunt Dilla from the office and left a cemetery number & told her to have Johnny call & ask for "Mr. Graves." She got to worrying for fear it was important and called them to tell them where to find John. When she found out it was a cemetery it began to dawn on her that it was an April Fool joke.

This old car shakes worse than a bronco.

Don't worry about me Mom. I took some powdered rhubarb root & cream of tartar and it cleaned me out fine. I've been keeping my "eliminator" open ever since. That's Aunt Dilla's pet name for it now.

I wonder if Emmet will finish getting married any better than Milton & George. They aren't any speedier about it than I am. I'm not taking any second hand men (Don't worry!). Aunt Josie always says every old goof is "lovely." Whew!

Myrtle

P.S. I hope to come up home for two weeks this summer, when I have saved up a little money.

Mpls
April 3 - 29

Girlie,

Carr is to stay at lake this summer & look after things. Told me he thinks of you often but never gets at writing letters. Says he came near writing time of Valentine.

I intend to stay Mpls till at least June or July. I will be getting a little art work each week make a few dollars. Dad never saves money and won't let me.

Orvis definitely wants to sail for home this spring, but Dad has not got the money yet. He has had a hard time at Duluth. The wholesalers tried to make him let them have what he has coming on his own deals to pay debts Paul has made. Had a big row. Dad told them he'd not be a dog for that store any longer so they finally agreed to meet at T-K tomorrow and decide what is to be done. Wheeler wants to work on cash and Geo. S. to run it but Dad wants to sell so I don't know how it will turn out. Perhaps when Dad gets to doing better he will let me have a chance to save a little. Ought to have learned his lesson anyway. All I can do is pray and I guess God gets tired of me doing that.

I have a headache today. Too much open window last nite. It's above my bed and Dad wants it open. He wants my bed instead of Murphy but is too short.

Mom

INTRODUCING
TAMARACK
MINNESOTA

Aitkin County, a Deep, Rich Black Loam, Clay Subsoil Area for Diversified Farming, Dairying and Stock Raising—the 1,165,691 Acres of Land Have Been Divided Into 1,348 Farms—Six Operating Money-Making Creameries in 1925 Had 2,333 Patrons, Owning 5,050 Dairy Cows, Manufacturing 1,132,367 Pounds of Butter and Paid Farmer-Dairymen in Butterfat Checks $414,950.27—the Increase of These Creameries From 1925 to 1928 Has Been 20 Per Cent Each Year—A Rich Hinterland in Soil for Big Crop Yields—Tamarack Is in the Making and Has a Bright Future, Full of Promise.

IDEAL OPPORTUNITIES

By JOHN A. MONGER

...anding the world-wide ...riculture since 1920, espe- ...e Middle West, Minnesota ...head in farm home mak- ...fied farming, dairying, ...l stock raising. This is ...o in Aitkin county, the ...il hinterland tributary to ...ality of Tamarack, with ...loped, modernly-equipped ...ributary chain of soul-in- ...s, for recreation, health ....population.

twelve miles of Tamarack, the progressive, friendly gateway to all of these lakes and resorts, on Trunk Highway No. 2 and State Aid Road No. 6. These are ideal waiting opportunities, only forty-five miles from Duluth via Trunk Highway No. 2, that will be paved within another year. Then there is the Northern Pacific short line from Duluth—Tamarack and Twin Cities. Indeed, it should be the ambition of every tourists to own a lake site and cottage on one of the beautiful Tamarack lakes, for health and pleasure.

...EALTH AND POPULATION.

...e First State bank of Tamarack ...ed its doors for business on Sept. ...1913, and during all the sixteen ...s has been faithful to its deposi- ...s. While many other banks have ...ed, the First State has grown and ...ospered, having deposits of $75,000 ...some wealth for a village of 165 ...opulation, U. S. census of 1920.

...Wayside Creamery, Tamarack, from ...ay 19, 1928, to Jan. 1, 1929, manu- ...actured 71,056 pounds of butter and ...paid 118 farmer-dairymen for butter- ...fat $28,536.93 — figures that will...

PAUL N. HELLER,
Manager Nelson-Heller Co.; mayor Tamarack, Minn.

Of the many public-spirited citizens of Tamarack and Aitkin county, none stands higher than Mayor Paul N. Heller, a pioneer merchant of eleven years' standing, manager of Nelson-Heller company's general merchandise store since it was incorporated for $50,000 in 1918. A man of few words, but a progressive business man, town builder and a promoter of farm home building. A man of wide vision. One reason why Tamarack occupies such an important place among the municipalities of the Northland.

FIRST STATE BANK,
Average deposits, $75,000;
Tamarack, Minn.

On Sept. 15, 1913, the First State bank of Tamarack was opened for business in its own banking house, size 24x60 feet, a commodious building with modern fixtures, cash vault and storage vault in basement. The opening of the First State was a red letter day in the history of Tamarack. The capital is $10,000; surplus, $3,000; average deposits, $75,000. Pays 4 per cent interest on time deposits; writes all kinds of insurance; makes commercial collections; pays taxes for non-residents and extends liberal accommodations to the business men and farmers alike, compatible with sound banking. The deposits are fully covered by indemnity insurance. For the past sixteen years the First State bank of Tamarack has been open for business, while many of the other banks in the state have been forced to close for lack of funds or frozen assets. The First State has a record that J. P. Brenner should take pride in, certainly its depositors do. The officers are: Charles H. Gustafson, president; H. J. Friestad, vice president; J. P. Brenner, cashier; M. A. Messner, assistant cashier.

Mr. Brenner owns and operates an eighty-acre farm, forty-five acres of which are under cultivation, in barley, potatoes,...clover. He sp...

MARCUS NELSON,
A famous Tamarack Booster.

Marcus Nelson is president of Nelson-Heller company, dealers in general merchandise, established in 1918. In 1920 Mr. Nelson established a tie sawmill, employing twenty-five men in the mill, and during the logging season 125. These industries laid the foundation that has made Tamarack such a dependable municipality. The timber having been logged off, the mill was put out of commission. Mr. Nelson is now engaged in the real estate business, with offices in the Metropolitan Bank building, Minneapolis, but he retains his interest in Tamarack, its lake shore sites and farm lands, with a summer cottage on Sandy lake. Mr. Nelson is a booster for Tamarack lake sites and farm lands. A hail fellow well met, one in a thousand. Here's ho, Marcus.

TAMARACK'S VILLAGE OFFICERS.
Few, if any, municipalities in the state have had a more representative class of citizens elected to fill the important positions of the village. They have been unselfish men, giving their time and money to make Tamarack an attractive place to live and do business in. That is why it has made progress, instead of lagging behind.
Paul N. Heller, mayor.
Hanna Duerr, clerk.
Irlene Kelly, treasurer.
Councilmen: R. E. Maron, Charles ...son, J. L. Cayo.

Mpls
April 20-29

Darling Myrtle,

Was a drunk guy at my door yesterday noon. He wanted to see landy lady and I told him she was on roof throwing snow off. So he tried to get in my room but I pushed him out and locked the door. He'd been drinking could tell by smell but might not been so shot as he acted.

Dad got word Marion's brother-in-law lives on our old farm now. First Nat'l Aitkin still owns it.

Dad not home yet must be doing a little business. He should be here soon as I promised bean soup with a little boiled ham & bacon. He always likes meat but I can easy do without - vegetables, fruit & bread o.k. by me.

Mom

P.S. I think you have catarrh of the bowels. I expect 2 or 3 quarts of Bulgarian buttermilk would be a good diet for you. No need to do much cooking then either. I just love it so much Dad always says must be alcohol in it.

Mpls
May 1-29

Darling Myrtle,

Was a big gun fight last nite in next block but can't find out what it was about. A doz. shots fired maybe more. You ought to have heard the women in the bldg. scurry for this side. I think the landy lady ducked under her window. I wanted to go out and see it but thot I better use a little sense. ha. ha.

Went to see another picture was a good clean show and funny. The Lagoon is called Uptown now. They want all Lake St. called that. It's been fixed up and has about 20 swell lookers dressed up to help people out of their cars. Putting on the dog some. ha. ha.

Mom

Camp Nichols, P.I.
May 5th, 1929

Myrtle,

Hard to believe I soon will be sailing for the States. I wonder sometimes what it will be like to see white girls everywhere again. I've spoken to less than a dozen white women in over a year, all of them married or like my two missionary friends, old maids. Here you will see one white girl and ten thousand brown ones. I think I'll ride around in an armored car with the key hid and guards to keep me in till I get acclimated. I don't want to be too susceptible. Huh?

Looks like I'll be going to Franklin College, Ind. in Sept. I can't handle Stanford financially. Was good enough for many Barnetts before me & should be able to live pretty cheap, maybe stay with a relation in exchange for odd jobs.

Orv

Mpls
May 29-29

My dear Myrtle,

I am all upset. I got a cable from Orvis that he could not make boat unless he had the discharge money at once. I have not been able to locate Marcus. I tried to get him to go after Tingdale last week but Marcus is getting like his father - all time in world. Way they see to business is a fright.

Mom

P.S. We are tired of these big apartments. People tear around all nite. On Monday I am to spend the day house hunting. When are you going to Sandy Lake?

RADIOGRAM
World Wide Wireless
Via Radio Corporation Of The Philippines
18KMMNV

MINNEAPOLIS MINN 22 6
TO: SERGEANT ORVIS
    NELSON 6 PHOTO SECTION
CAMP NICHOLS MANILA
MONEY SENT TODAY CABLE WHEN SHIP SAILS
    MARCUS NELSON

MAY 31 1929
9 39 AM

Orvis' two missionary friends.

4009 Nokomis Ave So., Mpls
June 25-29

Girlie,

Marcus came back from Sandy a few days after you left. He brought his & Carr's wash back and what a sight. Using soft coal & Carr is none to clean to start with. Dad let Mrs. Alfred Anderson take my oil stove so I suppose its goodbye to it. He is always so generous with my stuff but what a "howl" he put up because I gave the Indians some old clothes he'd not worn for 25 years. ha.

My cleaning job is awful hard work and I want to quit but I can't afford it. Dad plans to drive for Tingdale's weekends. Go to Sandy on Mondays and stay till Friday each week. If he will do that he will get a rest and I won't get so lonesome here.

Mom

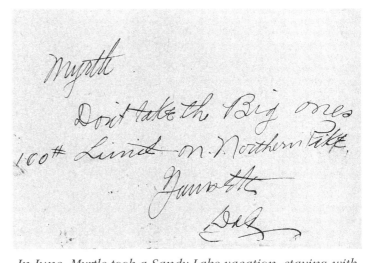

In June, Myrtle took a Sandy Lake vacation, staying with the Alfred Anderson's at their Prairie River Bridge Store. Marcus sent her this note from Minneapolis.

Mpls
July 18-29

Darling Myrtle,

I was surprised to get a letter today from the Philippines, from Miss Grbst, one of Orvis' missionary friends. It was a lovely letter about my son. She said he was an unusual boy and they sure enjoyed his visits. She said she was so surprised to find a young man so interested in missions and that he was a loyal son of a loyal mother. He spoke she said of all his folks but of me most tinderly. Well, I had to get such dim eyes I could not read had to rest for awhile. I surely have tried to raise my children right and I guess God must get tired of me for asking so much that he keeps them pure and fine.

They are cementing our alley. I wish you could see one of young guys who drives the little car that hauls sand & cement to mixer. He has just sleeveless underwear and his arms are the berries. A lovely tan that most girls give her eyes to own.

Hope to hear from the kid in Calif. next day or so.
Mom

San Francisco, Calif.
July 21st, 1929

Myrtle,

Believe me the good old U.S.A. feels mighty nice! Had a pretty nice voyage over even if we did buck heavy seas from Japan to Honolulu. We were delayed one day leaving Nagasaki by a typhoon. I did not get sick, rather enjoyed the added motion involved.

Last night I attended my first Talkie, "The Idle Rich," at the new Fox Theater. I enjoyed it all the way through. Had no idea what it would be like.

Get discharged next Saturday. I don't know just when I'll see you, will be awhile on the road. I am sharing costs with another discharged soldier who is heading East and has a car.
Orv

Franklin, Ind.
Aug 3rd 1929

Husband Marcus & Son Orvis,

My Father's death has been very hard. He was sick 3 days before a Dr. was called too late to save him. Dr. gave him something at last to stop convulsions. Was 87 years old. I rec'd your letter. I am alright in daytime but do not sleep much.

Myrtle & her dentist friend are coming tomorrow. He is nicest boy friend she has had yet. Has a fine Nash car is large fine looking man 26 years old.

Glad your car is nice Marcus and thanks dear for such a lovely letter. Be so glad to see you both.
Love, Mom and Mamie

Myrtle and possibly her dentist friend.

Sandy Lake
Aug 24-29

Girlie,

Expect you & Orvis been getting in a lot of catching up and I know everyone in Ind. was looking forward to seeing him again. Orvis, have you talked to college yet?

Dad & Carr put a new roof on my front porch as it was in pitiful condition. I made a jelly roll for dinner a large one and they et it all and called it fine. I have to make a cobbler most every day. They run me ragged with housework & cooking.

Mom

Franklin
Sept 3, 1929

Folks,

My credits from Hamline are O.K. Franklin College told me I would be starting in Mathematics not engineering but that is all right I guess. Must make the best of things.

I told Myrtle to telegram Dad I'll need a hundred right away and fifty more next week. Dad, send it to Myrtle at Aunt Dilla's.

Orvis

Indypls
Sept 5th, 1929

Dad & Mom,

Orvis wore the white suit he bought in P.I. today & sure looked nifty. He has been scurrying around setting up an aerial photo business to earn money for school. Plans to sell pictures of farms, factories, town plaza's, etc. He has turned into a real go-getter. Starts at Franklin College on Sept. 25th.

One of the girls quit yesterday so the Rockwood office is overloaded with work again. Beginning to sound like a broken record, eh? Seems like I've been here forever.

Myrtle

Ert Nay harvesting wheat.

3443 Washburn Ave. No. Mpls
Sept 30-29

My dear Myrtle,

Orvis has settled in at Aunt Mag & Uncle Ert's. Will milk cows and do hired work for board & room. Their place about 14 miles from college. He is going to try & get hold of a car.

Orvis said he would not go out for football but Ert would have none of it. Said if Orvis had to let chores go O.K. could make it up later but did not want him to let the chance go by. Ert is good hearted.

Orvis is to team up with a man name of Wally Ensminger who will do flying while Orvis takes pictures. They will work on speculation only way can do it but Orvis says has lots of people already interested & is sure can make money. Be good as Dad has very little to spare.

Too bad times are so hard about work. Is a lot of real trouble here. Won't pay much and union men mostly on strike. You won't know town. I get balled up myself so many new bldgs. Wonder where they get the money to build it all.

Wish could give you a piece of my bread - black of course. I eat warm with honey. Remember how Colonel King loved warm bread with brown sugar and lots of butter?

Mom

Indypls
Nov 15, 1929

Mom & Dad,

Sorry about that blue letter yesterday. It was a pretty heavy double blow.

I've decided it's just as well Rockwood's let me go. I needed something to shake me from my rut. The big shots there are sure shook up over the stock market.

I would like to come to Mpls and stay with you as soon as I can. All of a sudden, I feel I need a significant change of scenery - am tired of the people and place and am homesick for Minnesota.

And as for men, I'm on sabbatical!

Myrtle

Rockwood Pulley Co.
Indypls
December 1, 1929

Hello Murdo,

Well, my dear I am glad you arrived at your destination without any mishaps. I'll bet you had a big time on the bus. I expect you are already looking for work, or maybe you're just taking it easy for awhile? How do you like your folk's house?

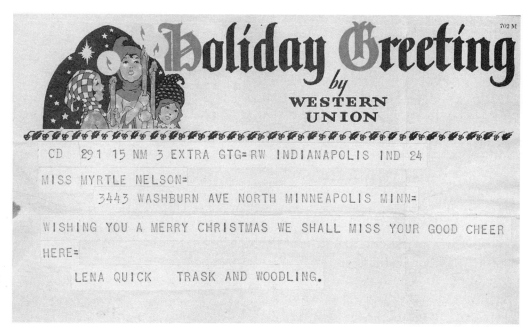

1929 Christmas greeting from the Rockwood gang.

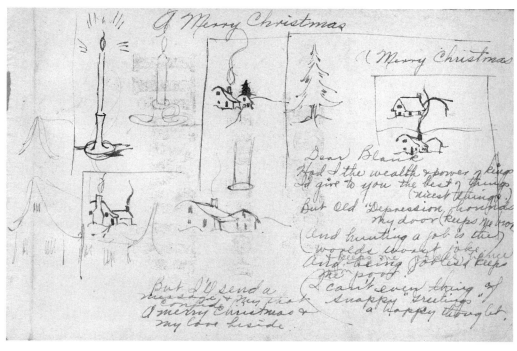

First draft of Myrtle's 1929 Christmas card (years ago it was common to make your own). Here is a part of her thoughts: "Dear Blank Had I the wealth & power of kings I'd give to you the best of things but old "Depression" hounds my door (Keeps me broke) (and hunting a job is the worlds worst joke) and being jobless keeps me poor I can't even think of snappy 'Greetings,' a happy thought."

So your last interview with the dignified John came out fairly easy? Too bad that life scars one so much. I know - I've been disappointed to, so I can feel sorry for John - but on the other hand I cannot and decidedly do not blame you. It is a good thing you decided as you did for as you say, "better now than after." There is too much of that sort of thing carried to the Minister that ends with the Judge.

I have been working hard & fast this week. The traveling auditor from the New York Office is making out his reports and, of course, I'm getting the burnt end of the cigar to smoke.

Yours forever,

Jennie Eudaly

Indypls
12-19-29

My dear Miss Nelson,

This is your old friend-boy "Gilly" in reply to your nice letter. Glad you are having a good time and getting acquainted but I certainly do not like your going out with Big Swedes what pats Girls on knees. That is a thing unheard of here.

We (the Gang and myself) were all at the Crystal Saturday night and had a pretty good time until old Battle Axe barred us from the hall. It is a long story and, of course, a woman's fault. We were back in the corner as per usual not doing anything out of the way except loving the Girls a little and the Girls setting on our laps when who should appear but the Villain. "Ah," she cried, twisting her moustache. "Caught at last!" And so we were told not to come back and the story is continued until next Saturday night.

Jen was there but must have gone home before this happened as it was at the close of the dance. I had to give her a raken down for having steady dates. I told her she shouldn't get interested in anybody but me.

My power is getting low and I will have to quit broadcasting, but if I was talking to you, how I could sling it.

Your friend, H. Gilley

P.S. Jennie says you have sworn off men. I bet you will recover.

Tamarack
Jan 3 1930

Uncle Marcus & Aunt Mamie,

Mamma sends her best. In regards to the sled, it wasn't us that wanted to buy it. It was Mr. John Larson. And he says the price is reasonable enough but he hasn't the cash now.

I suppose Orvis is back in school again, and how is Myrtle getting along, has she found work yet?

I guess work is kind of scarce this winter, and there's not much money in circulation either. There may be lots in circulation but the circles can't be very big for they don't hit Tamarack.

Your nephew, Maurice Nelson

Rockwood Pulley Co.
Jan 10th, 1930

Pal Murdo,

It doesn't seem possible that my beaux Gorman and I should be so gay and you so blue. I hope when you get this you will have recovered some of your old gay spirits and be yourself again. Cheer up - your red-headed milkman may be a good provider.

Any more exciting job interviews like the Be-Spatted Lawyer? That cigarette holder took the cake!

Cold as blazes here. I nearly froze my knees on the way to work. I wished for one of those knee-patting Swedes you told me about. Ha. Ha.

Yours till longer skirts,

Jennie

AERIAL PHOTOGRAPHS   **MOSAIC MAPPING**

INDIANA AIR VIEWS

SHELBYVILLE, INDIANA

Feb 1st, 1930

Dad & all,

Mighty nice to hear you talking on the 'phone last night. It was a pleasant surprise to me. Uncle Ert & Aunt Mag got almost as big a kick out of things as I did. We sat up quite awhile afterwards, talking. I expect these farmers around here enjoyed it too, for no doubt a gang were listening. They always do, especially on a late call. That's probably the longest call the Marietta operator every handled so the news will spread. You've about made yourself famous over night. Believe me, I appreciate all you, Mom, & Myrtle are doing for me.

Finals next week. Already had my English so just have Algebra, Chemistry, & Economics.

Many thanks to Dennis when you see him. I can't say how much I appreciate his gift of money. Tell him I will write a long letter.

Bye, Orv

P.S. Sold two air photos to the Indy Star. How do you like my new stationery?

1202 Hoyt Ave
Indypls
Feb 21, 1930

Myrt,

I was thinking of you so much I got out the souvenirs of my "Rockwood days" gone by. I found that little telegram you sent with my going away gift. It brought tears to my eyes. I recognize a friend when I have one, and you've certainly been one to me.

So you're a cost clerk at Bloom Brothers. I'm glad you seem to like it.

I told Bud what you said about triplets. He said, "Thanks for the compliment, ask her if she thinks I'm that good a man." No Myrtle, there's none on the way, and married 8 months. I 'spose my Rockwood friends are disappointed because I'm not going to have at least one before my nine months are up.

I told Bud several things you wrote in your letter and he said, "She sure missed her calling because she should have been a journalist." I think so too because I just love to read your letters - they sound just like a book and you're so original.

Bud is not so sensitive about his size & still laughs when he tells people one of my friends told him he looked like he was going to give birth to a nation. He says, "You know she just has this way about her that she can say anything and it would sound alright." See, he admires you so much I'm afraid if I kick off you can just expect a proposal.

Love, Betty Gregg

Rockwood Pulley Co.
March 8th, 1930

Pal Murdo,

I was absolutely charmed by the manner in which you wrote about child-birth control, etc. Eh-he-he! Had so many spasms over it that my married sister had to be enlightened about the cause of all the mirth, so I let her laugh with me. I know you won't mind, because she could not even think of being rude about your letter. So have no fears, tho better not write that way to any Catholic girls you know, for Myrtle, they would have you burned at the stake!

Went with Peg to the Ohio to see "Her Unborn Child" which, as advertised, is "the sweetest story every told." Don't fail to see it. The title I'll admit is rank but the show is marvelous. I cried! Now I know you'll go, won't you?

Thank heavens my father has a little work now, but I don't have any idea how long it will last. Anyway it will help out oodles, no doubt. As long as I can add my ten dollars a week my folks are glad to have me at home.

My dear, my body is in a most frightful state. I wrote you about my bum feelings which I thot might be caused from my should be approaching period, but which failed to put in an appearance even up until Friday. I've never experienced any pains or delays to speak of in all of my "career," so 2 days ago I went to Dr. and he said I've a misplaced something or other, and proceeded to treat the affected parts and gave me a very bitter green medicine. I've no kick coming - as it produced the desired effect.

So much for that. I'll be getting fired for writing personal letters instead of doing my business correspondence.

With lots of love, hugs, kisses, chocolate drops, coca colas, and Lydia E. Pinkham's,

Jen

Franklin College, Ind.
March 19, 1930

Dad,

Got your welcome letter this morning. Always glad to find any from you waiting for me. Also had the usual one from Mom.

The meat arrived O.K. I put it in the icebox for now. Is no question but what it's O.K.; that lard is a great preservative.

I've been running at B in all my subjects, even in Trigonometry. I expect I'll slip off a bit, for it is naturally getting more difficult as we go along. Pretty hot in Chemistry and Advanced Composition, as usual. Also taking 3 hours of Economics, and two hours each of Short Story and Physics of the air, otherwise known as Meteorology. Total of 17 prepared credit hours; the average college requirement is 14 prepared and 1 unprepared.

I decided to put off getting initiated in Kappa Delta Rho as I need the money. Say, if Myrtle can come down in June she might be here when I get my football sweater.

Orv

P.S. I sure could use a five spot. My meal ticket is punched out & I'm flat again.

Orvis (middle of rear row) eventually joined Kappa Delta Rho fraternity.

Hinckley, Minn.
May 9, 1930

Moitie Dear!

My sinuses are worse over here than they ever were at Grandy. Hope they clear up before our trip to Indiana starts.

I have nothing here to do any mileage calculations on but an Atlas and as each state is separate it is somewhat hard. I will get some road maps when I get into town. As to how far our money will go, $65 or $70 ought to be enough. The car is insured for accident and if anything goes wrong and the two of us get out of cash and stranded we can telegraph Joe for aid. Of course he might not want me so badly but I am quite sure he would want the car back. I believe he thinks it a little foolhardy for two girls to go alone but he has not said anything about it to me.

I will have to steer clear of your mother cause I'm a terrible smoker now and you told me once she didn't approve. It is a rotten habit though a great consolation to me this winter. You never would have imagined me getting that habit 3 yrs. ago would you? Imagine sitting in Mrs. Oman's "settin" room smoking a "Lucky!"

I'm for taking wash dresses - Heaven save us from knickers; they always make me think of old maid schoolmarms on a pleasure jaunt. Can you imagine old maid schoolmarms having any pleasure? I suppose it would consist of a series of fossilized squeals and virginal cries as each butterfly and petting party crosses their path.

I must tell you a joke; it isn't exactly dirty so here 'tiz:

An old Irish woman, very ignorant, moved into the city. A circus came to town and one of the elephants got away. The old woman looked out her back window and there was the elephant pulling up things out of her garden. She had never seen an elephant before and didn't know what it was so she called up the Police:

"Sure theres a quare lookin baste in the garden pulling up cabbages wid his tail."

"What is he doing with them?" asked the Chief.

She answered, "Aw don't be axin personal questions."

Love, Carol Newman

"Whispering Pines" on Round Lake.

they had about tapped the well dry in Indiana.

Floyd Cyrus & Nort Kelley just came out to see Orvis and of course the boys are having a fine time. Carr was so glad to see O. The old man has 88 pines planted on "Breeze Hill." Will not take any pay, can you beat it. He has kept hold of most the money he got from 1918 fire claim.

Orvis is worried about having enough money to go back to college does not think he can do it. I don't know what to do except give money & have none to give, and he has three more years to go.

Mom

P.S. Sorry Bloom Bros. had to let you go girlie. They like everyone else can't pay for help they need.

Mpls
June 25-30

Darling son,

Is little news. Girls won their kittenball game last nite because other side did not have all it's best players so Myrtle says anyway. She was late getting home as they like to go somewheres afterward.

Dad says Phil & Elsie Barott are starting up a "resort" on their place on Round Lake. Are to call it "Whispering Pines" - fishing, swimming, camping, etc. He says the 4 stores in Tamarack are doing business but with no profit to speak of. Collections bad. People north of town are hard up because are still timber minded. South of town they are milking cows and prosperous.

Mom

P.S. I hardly see Dad anymore.

Sandy Lake
Sept 3-30

Dearest Myrtle,

Day before yesterday, Orvis & Wally Ensminger landed their plane in field south of Doc Snader's Maternity Hospital & got Percy Cayo at garage to run them up to Sandy. Caused quite a stir in Tamarack as many had not seen a plane close up before. They were in sky all day yesterday taking photos, was a nice day. This morning they drove around selling them. Did O.K. will go out tomorrow again. Said

Orvis and Wally on the job.

Franklin College Athletic Department
Sept 12, 1930

Dear Nelson,

Received your letter yesterday and was very glad of your determination to return to school. You had us worried.

41

Orvis took this picture during the September trip home.
State Bank of Tamarack in foreground, Nelson's store above it, feed mill to the left.

Mpls
October 22, 1930

I spoke to Dean Powell and, though somewhat reluctant, he looked at your records and has agreed to allow you to take an average of 21 hours per semester (plus summer school) in order for you to finish your degree in three years instead of four. You are also approved to pursue a Math major with a minor in Education. I agree it is wise to get a teaching certificate should it come to pass you are unable to attain your goal of Army Aviator.

Also, good news - the faculty has approved your loan. Mr. Burton will be glad to arrange for payments at your convenience. His only request is that you settle by the end of each semester.

Now that everything is settled, I shall expect to see you quickly heading south and will watch every plane that comes over hoping you are in it. We have a bang-up schedule this year - Butler, Wabash, DePauw, Earlham, etc. and we need our Center (#30) to hurry back as practice has already started.

E.B. Wagner
Athletic Director

Dear _____:

You are cordially invited to a costume dance on Halloween, Friday October 31st, given by the well known Grave Diggers Union of Coffin Hall, Eleven South Casket Street. Take cemetery car to the dance, or if preferred a hearse will call at your residence.

Tickets may be purchased from the undertakers at the deadly price of 25 cents. Positively, no credit. Orphans accompanied by parents admitted free of charge.

Refreshments will be served by the Embalmers Cafe featuring blood punch & head cheese sandwiches. Murder will be committed to amuse the children. The Pep for the evening will be supplied by the Shroud Association of Crepe Hangers, plus at midnight the Corpse Quartet will moan the Dying Song. Door prize is a complimentary cadaver supplied by the University Medical School.

Please do not disappoint us by being there.
Mournfully yours,
A. Skeleton (a.k.a. Myrtle Nelson)

34061 Tribune, Mpls
Monday, January 5th, 1931

Sir:

With reference to your Sunday employment ad, I would like to apply for the position. I have extensive experience in both manual & automatic switchboards. I am a speed typist and have experience in general office work. You will also note I have taken many correspondence courses at the American Business College.

I live at home, am 26 years old, and not married. As it is necessary I work, I am willing to start at your figure.

For your convenience, I enclose a recent photograph, with stamp attached. Please kindly return it if you are not interested.

May I have an interview? My telephone number is Hyland 4567.

Myrtle B. Nelson

3443 Washburn Ave. Mpls
Jan 29-31

Mr. Martin Tingdale
Dear Brother-In-Law,

Marcus has disappeared and I have not been well enough to come down so will tell you how it is with me.

I get a little money from farm land my Pa left me and along with my cleaning work had saved up $600 - and had intended to put it against the Lake note we owe you coming due. Had I known what was going on with Marcus I never would have give that money to him but he insisted & now it and him seems to have vanished.

I can't bear to lose the lake so better go ahead on a new 5 year note for $1200. The lower the interest rate the better, of course. You had said 7%. There are no back taxes on it, as I have managed to get work somewhere even tho I had to go out house cleaning and work like a slave to 8 at nite. Marcus claims he has money coming from you tho not due yet and if that is so why can't you pay it now - put it up on credit to him & then lessen amount of mortgage note. Do not send anything for Marcus to sign but give the papers to me for I intend to see what is done from now on my self.

I see no reason why you cannot fix it up to make Marcus and Mrs. Williams pay me back that $600. He is liable to run off with this adventuress or get sick and unable to do anything as he tells me he has heart trouble and is taking medicine for it. If he were to die he has not enough for funeral expenses, and my girl can find no work and of course Orvis needs all he can make. I cannot depend on them, you know most young folks now do well enough to support themselves. Then Orvis work is dangerous and he is liable to get killed or crippled anytime. He can't afford a parachute and anyway he flys too low to take pictures to do any good.

Martin, if you have any feeling at all for a human being in distress then compel Marcus to give me back that money & I will give it to you and can make the mortgage for only $600. I do not know if I will ever be able to work all day any more because of way muscles are cut from my arms. I am bravely doing what I can.

Very truly,
Mamie Nelson

Tingdale Bros., City
Feb. 7th, 1931

Mamie,

As I told you on the phone today I have sold your lake mortgage to Dolph Bezoier. If at the end of the five years the time payments have been satisfactorily made, a warranty deed for the 8 acre lake property will be issued by him in your children's names.

I am sorry that nothing better for you could be arranged on this matter. You must understand that I can do nothing with Marcus & that in these very difficult times business must remain business.

Martin Tingdale

Franklin College
April 28, 1931

Folks,

I was elected to "Blue Key" Junior-Senior Honorary Fraternity for men last night. Is a national organization for outstanding students. I was also elected a member of the Interfraternity Council. Not so bad, eh?

Orv

Wesley Church Employment Service
Mpls
May 21, 1931

Miss Myrtle Nelson
C/O P. Schlampp & Sons
City
Dear Miss Nelson:

Your letter received with fee enclosed. Thank you. I do hope your place will last some time yet, for work is terribly scarce, very little except housework coming in right now, and not much hope for better for some weeks to come. But you are welcome to come back to me as soon as you are through, and I assure you I'll do my best to help you again.

Mrs. Ida Kent, Manager

Mpls
5/27/31

Mr. Marcus Nelson,

I understand you are going into the lunchroom business at your camp on Sandy Lake. I am not doing any thing & if you have any thing or know of any thing let me know. How about a job at your lake as helper in the kitchen? I have always been a good meat & vegetable cook & have been doing all the cooking home for the past few months. Will work cheap.

D.L. Fairchild

Franklin College
June 1, 1931

Folks,

Summer school starts in Louisville on June 11 and I am set up there o.k. Plan to drive down early that morning.

With their numbers growing, hunters & fishermen soon tired of the rough camps, (above), leading men like Marcus to provide more "civilized" dining (below).

Dad, I need money awful bad. There is still $50 from last semester due. Then this semester is $131 and the Fraternity bill I guess you know. This all has to be paid by the end of the 1st week of this month. You'll recall I wrote about all this a few weeks ago.

I know this adds up to quite a wad of money but it's really almost a year's tuition. I have no credit in Louisville and cannot let go of the $43 I've saved, for I have no other way to pay my way down there. Besides, If I don't get the money to Franklin soon it means I won't be able to graduate next year, if ever. I'll be another whole year behind, and my name will be mud.

Must run, Wally got a last minute job - pays $5. Please see what you can do.

Orv

119 W. Barbee
Louisville, Ky.
June 23, 1931

Folks,

Got letter from school saying they received a substantial payment and all is O.K. They, of course, want the balance paid as soon as possible but they were friendly and understanding. Whew! A relief, thanks a million Dad. I can still use a little help on the fraternity bill but they can wait a while longer if it is necessary.

School is forging ahead - having some fun now that I can enjoy it! I like the teachers; they are so full of their subjects they make it interesting for us.

School is out Aug 8th and I'll certainly will be glad to come up home for a month and forget everything.

Orv

Mpls
June 28 - 31

Mr. D.A. Carr, Sandy Lake

Carr -

If Marcus has not left tell him to come down before the third. Please write and tell me what he aims to do. Time is short and we have to refinance the house here.

Also if he can't come after me let me know so I can go to work here. Tell him to send Orvis a five to tide him over.

Hope you are having nice weather & the fishermen are having good luck so they will want to come back next year. It's been so hot here we are about melted. Most people are trying to sleep any place but in beds. Any place to get a breath of air.

Myrtle and I had your radishes this noon and you should have seen us eat them. They were so crisp and good. Had both tables shoved together and kept the dish passing from one end to the other. There were two left when we got up from the table and I cabbaged them.

It's sprinkling a little tonight so maybe it will be a little cooler. Now it is thundering and the radio is so full of static am afraid we won't hear Amos and Andy.

M.N.

Orvis & Rozena Whitesides, voted "the most popular girl in the Alva Neal high school, Franklin, by the student body."

"Nelson's Camp"
Sandy Lake
Saturday Evening, Aug 8th 1931

Myrtle,

Oh we kids are having a great time at your lake. Everyone was so sad you could not get up but of course you could not pass up that temp. offer when you have had so little work.

Your Dad dropped us off Thursday early afternoon and we went swimming & then fishing. We caught a bunch of sunfish. Boy! It was fun. They were biting beautifully. It was very hot and I had only my bathing suit on all day. After cleaning our fish, we went to town where I bought a bottle of olive oil, by that time badly needed.

That evening we had a big beach fire, sang with the ukulele, and roasted marshmallows & listened to readings by various members of the party. We had just loads of fun.

Today took a long boat ride; explored all points

Enjoying Life At Big Sandy Lake.

of interest along the lake; ate some stolen green apples; and were blown ashore on some rocks at the far end. Last of all we went out on the island and examined some potatoes an unknown agriculturalist has planted out there. It looked so odd to see a domesticated plant growing there with all the wild stuff.

Late this afternoon we had a little accident. I felt so sorry for little Jean. Yesterday I had been teaching her how to row. She kept time so well, and dipped her oar so precisely for a youngster. She was very proud. Well, today she couldn't wait to take Ed & I out to troll for northern pike and she slipped somehow, fell backward into the bottom of the boat, and lost both oars. Hurt her back terribly it seemed. We were so startled we just let the oars drift away.

Jean burst into tears at what had happened - scared to death. "Oh - I want my mother to come and take me away from here!" We paddled back to the oars with our hands, the current helping somewhat. By the time we got back to your beach she had calmed down & we were all relieved it wasn't any worse. She's still sore but not hurt as bad as we first thought. Such excitement!

Tomorrow morning we are going to attend services at the Christian Church at Tamarack. Mrs. Doctor Snader heard friends of Myrtle's were at the lake & brought us out a basket of sandwiches and cake, then invited us to services. She was very sweet. We will leave for Mpls right after church.

Great time honey, thx so much. See you soon!
Elsie Borg

A Bird's-Eye View of Modern Aitkin

ABOVE is reproduced the first airplane picture of modern Aitkin, downtown, taken by Orvis Nelson, formerly of Tamarack, who secured a number of excellent views of the community during the recent Aitkin County Fair.

Mr. Nelson was trained in aerial photography while a member of an aviation unit of the United States navy. He is offering his pictures for sale, and is also taking orders from dealers for postcards.

The picture above is taken from the northern end of Minnesota avenue looking south, with the New Foley Hotel and the Aitkin Armory included among buildings clearly shown in the background. The large building to the right in the foreground is Larson's Store.

The cars lined up along the streets reveal a typical every-day trading crowd—not a Saturday crowd. Aitkinites will be proud of the metropolitan aspects of their little city as revealed here.

Sandy Lake
Aug 13-31

Dearest Myrtle,

Dad drove home from Duluth over the new paved Thru Highway #2 or #210 they are to call it - said was a fine ride all the way to T-K. He been staying more at home lately.

Store is about out of debt & Dad is planning on getting out piling and ties this winter.

Mom

Sandy Lake
Oct 28 1931

My Dear Orvis & Myrtle,

Dilla's letter said you arrived fine and are having a good time. It has been pouring rain here for days seems. Myrtle I enclose all your mail. I put your old tent Orvis up to protect my bed as roof is so leaky. Marcus never did get around to fixing rest of it even tho all materials sitting in corner. It's letting up now some.

I guess Hughes & party will leave if can't fish. I don't see how they enjoyed fishing as it has been so cold. Mrs. Anderson said they come up to her house and warm up.

I made four towels for hands out of cement sacks for Aunt Annie's. They are out of so much. I picked up some old socks and underwear for Ernest & Maurice. She is glad to get anything.

Am ready to go down to Mpls but I got to watch about the place here and see that man Bezoier to get the coupons off the mortgage, for I do not trust Dad or Tingdale either one. Josie be right in it too if she can get her $500 that Dad signed a note for time his Dad died.

Aunt Emma sure gets sore about way Dad & Josie & Christine settled up Grandpa Nielsen's estate. She kept him a year and Dad told her that was only visiting. She told me Grandpa was often very cruel to Grandma, treated her better in the old country. I was not too surprised. Said Grandma had a bible she lost when their house burned at Nelson Lake in 1894 Hinckley fire. Had been in Anderson family since the 16th Century & written on papers. I sure wish it had not burned up. I want you both to have some long visits with Grandma Nielsen and your Uncle Ole before they die and get a good idea of way it was & learn about your ancestors.

Love, Mom

Hinckley, Minn.
Dec 27th, 1931

Myrtle,

So pleased you are getting your Two Year Teaching Certificate. At least with Intermediate Grades you can get a paying job and with more choices than just with your First Grade. You should be in teaching anyway - you were good at it.

For heaven's sake, don't get discouraged just because you can't write your stories all at once. It takes time - you have to write them over and over. They always sound terrible at first. But I know you have talent for writing and I'll be disappointed in you if you don't do something with it sometime in your life.

Carol Newman

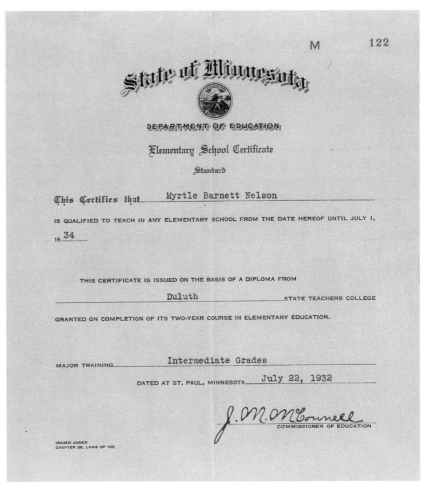

Myrtle's two-year graduation certificate from Duluth State Teachers College.

48

March 2, 1932.

To Whom it may concern:

Mr. Orvis Nelson has been an outstanding football player at Franklin College for three years, and in 1931 was an All-State center in the Indiana Conference.

Besides playing thru practically every game for two straight years, he has the record of having no bad passes at center during this period.

I attribute his effectiveness as a football player to the maintenance of unusual physical condition, and his determination.

In addition to his ability in athletics Nelson had the highest academic rating of all football men in the Conference in 1931 according to a report made by President Athearn of Butler University after a survey of the field.

Mr. Nelson will graduate with three years of study after earning his way thru college by aerial photography and I cheerfully recommend him in any of his undertakings.

Respectfully,

Roy E. Tillotson.

Director of Physical Education,
Football Coach.

Franklin College
March 3, 1932

Folks,

Lt. Goddard, my C.O. in the Philippines, wrote a friend in Washington about my application to Flight Training at Randolph Field, San Antonio, Texas. You see the Air Corps first makes you go there to what they call "A" and "B" (Basic) Stages for 8 and a half months before sending you on to the Advanced training at nearby Kelly Field for 3 and a half months (grand total one year). He gave me a good letter of recommendation, as did Dean Powell and Coach Tillotson. Coach gave me such a good one I was afraid to send it in.

It is awful hard to get an appointment; West Point men get preference and then there are just so many qualified boys from all over the country. Well, I will just have to do what I can and hope for the best.

Orvis

Tingdale Bros.
March 1, 1932

Marcus,

We have had a talk with Dr. Bemis and he stands very stubbornly for the game reserve all around Lake Margaret and Gull Lake. He believes it will help his business but he is wrong; it has killed all kinds of businesses around Lake Minnetonka. You cannot sell a piece of property there anymore. People do not want those game refuge signs, makes them afraid to go out with a gun and duck shoot.

You should know this will surely hurt Mrs. Williams' place. Of course, there is only one way to fight it and that is at the meeting, March 5th, in the farmer's room in the Court House in Brainerd, at 2:30 PM. So, I hope you will be there and give them a good talk against game reserves. Knowing your wide acquaintances around the State I thought you might be able to convince these people what is right.

Martin Tingdale

AITKIN REPUBLICAN
July 14, 1932

SANDY LAKE NEWS-
Mr. Orvis M. Nelson, son of Mr. and Mrs. Marcus Nelson, is at home with his parents after graduating with a degree from Franklin College, Indiana. After exhaustive physical, psychological, and academic examinations these past weeks, Orvis is pleased to announce that he has received word that he's been given a coveted appointment to the Air Corps Flying School and will be leaving for Texas in October.

Indypls
Sept 25, 1932

Aunt Mamie & Cousin Myrtle,
After the royal way in which you treated us at your lake, I think we owe you a vote of thanks. Everyone is raring to come again.

Myrtle, my impression of your friend Miss Elsie Borg is that she is a most attractive young lady. In fact, I think both you and she are too brilliant to be teaching in a "Jungle School," worthy though the neighborhood offspring may be. Isn't that funny your school is so close to where your father's development was on Lake Minnewawa.

You & Elsie seem to be pretty evenly matched as regards witty repartee, and quick comebacks. I think Gray must have had you two in mind when he wrote:

"Full many a flower is known to bloom unseen,
  and waste it's sweetness on the desert [jungle] air."
  Cousin Hiram Crandall

The Jungle School, an ungraded elementary school between Round Lake and Minnewawa.

Randolph Field
San Antonio, Texas
Oct. 17, 1932

Folks,
  Wow, first 2 days has been a whirl. Arrived by bus and 2 blue-clad upperclassmen laid into us before we got out the door & it has not stopped since. The ones with white arm bands are in charge of us "dodo's." You know, the flightless bird - that is suppose to be their idea of a joke. Anyway, these "upper class" boys wear blue name tags and we wear red. One of them, Mr. Dunlap, told us while still standing in front of the bus, "Gentlemen, I have only one piece of advice to give you. As long as you heed it you will have no trouble here. And this is - Keep your mouth shut and your alimentary tract open."

Orvis and the single-engine basic training airplane.

With my two years of Army experience I thought it would be easier than it is. They told us they have to give us three years of work in one and that less than forty five per cent of us will receive our wings even though each man has been hand picked by flight surgeons and a group of officers. Sure hope I can make it all the way thro.

I am in a room on the second floor of one of the barracks with 2 other boys. The food is excellent but we have to sit at attention & they don't give us much time to eat it!

Lights out. Letters gratefully appreciated!
Orv

Randolph Field
Thanksgiving Eve, 1932

Folks,

The day is about over and I've slept through most of it. We had a big dinner - you name it, we had it!

Been lovely flying last few days - the air clear & warm & smooth. I went through the usual routine of chandelles, spins, Lazy 8's, loops, steep banks, etc. Out 45 minutes alone (I soloed after six hours dual instruction - average is about eight) and then 45 minutes with my instructor practicing Pylon 8's. They are about the hardest thing I've had yet as it calls for such precision flying. You pick out two points on the ground & then come in and fly a complete circle around the first one, with your wing tip pointing at the point, and then roll out & put the other wing down on the other point and turn around it - then repeat the whole maneuver once again. It is hard to keep your bank regulated so as to keep the point "stuck" on a certain part of the wing. We fly it at 400 ft. above the ground and you always make your turn into the wind thus:

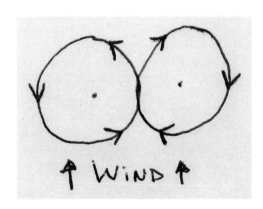

If I can learn to do them properly my hardest part of the first 4 months will be over.

We drew our solo helmets yesterday. Here-to-fore we have been wearing helmets with tubes going to ears for dual - our instructor could talk to us. For solo we have been taking the tubes out but the wind whistles so through the holes.

I am enclosing a few snaps which will give you an idea about the uniform. Those tags on my chest are name tags (Nelson, O.M.). We're well labeled you know.

Sounds like Myrtle is pleasing her clientele all right, but I knew she would. Teaching suits her.

I feel fine. I sure aim to stay and graduate if I can!

Bye - Orvis

Indypls
Dec 14, 1932

Myrtle,

So your brother never got married? The way the girls were crazy about him, I'd have thought he'd have been kid snatched by now.

I'm so glad you're teaching school again. I always thought you'd make a wonderful teacher. With a personality like yours, I'm sure the children will all love you. I imagine it takes a lot of patience with beginners, doesn't it? I'll sure have to broadcast the news over to Rockwood, so they'll sit up and take notice. I bet they'll turn green with envy. With your education and background, that was no place for you.

Saw Jennie last week for the first time in a while. She said it sounded like you were on with Jerry again and that you were coming down to visit him over Christmas vacation. I thought that was over ages ago. I am all ears and can't wait to hear what is going on??!!

Betty & Bud Gregg
P.S. Let us hope Roosevelt can figure a way to get people jobs. Lot's we know are scared of what he might do.

Sandy Lake
Dec 26-32

Girlie,

Glad you and Orvis got to Indypls o.k. honey. Wish I could have gone too but Dad wanted me here.

He is about over the flu seems to get it every year on a regular basis. He was out to Aunt Emma's and she gave us some coffee bread and a nice piece of pork they just killed. He cranky on account he wanted to look at some papers but left his "grief case" in Emma's car.

I staid with Marcus last nite and slept on Spike's bed (he is gone). Dad would not let me stay nite before last to keep up fires but he was glad to have me last nite. He could hardly walk 2 days ago. He may been scared he die alone but Dr. does not figure any danger of sudden death. He groaned a lot first part of nite but slept like a baby the rest. When I mail this I'll take water over to him. Hope Spike comes today as I've not much wood left.

Well, Dennis has finished your new little cabin on the hill. He wanted so bad to have it done so you could move in when got back from Indiana. Am happy as you will only be a few minutes up the path and we will not be bumping into each other arguing over who is boss. ha. ha.

Well I sure miss you and how! When you left seemed like the sun had gone down for good. I sure hope you children get along good and feel well. Hello from me to all.

Mom

My little Cabin on the Hillside Sandy Lake
Sunday, Jan 15th 1933

UNTITLED

I   The leaves are softly falling
            resting in their earthen bed,
      And bitter tears are calling
            to hopes forever dead.

II   A head is bowed as tears fall
            the eyes are sad and brown,
      And the silly little girl's heart
            with sorrow is cast down.

III   Oh yes - she richly deserves it -
            Tho' the lesson's hard to learn,
      She really cared for so very long
            Now her heart with yearning burns.

IV   And the other - the girl he cares for
            loves another, not he -
      But she uses him for a play thing
            Her duplicity he cannot see.

V   The little girl must keep the secret
            No other can ever know,
      That trust and dreams and happiness
            Were killed by a single blow.

VI   The leaves are softly falling
            resting in their earthen bed,
      her weeping, sad eyes calling
            After dreams forever dead.

Dedicated to the day dreams that made me happy but which I must put out of my mind in fairness to everyone concerned.
Myrtle B. Nelson

Hillside Cabin
March 12, 1933

Orv,

Mom is still on her "warm-up" Texas trip but will be coming back soon I think. Dad is running around the country as usual. He has been busy selling wood and lots - and is thick as thieves again with Tingdale.

President Roosevelt's "bank holiday" sure struck home. It doesn't look like the Tamarack bank will ever open again. It's awful for everyone over there. Carr says the Gustafson brothers - Charlie, Axel, & Oscar - have lost everything. All their money was in the bank and from what Dennis said the poor old batches were quite well off. I am just sick over it. I hope Dad didn't have much there - I don't think he did (He probably owes them!).

Looks like the "wets" are going to get their way, not just here but all over the country. Dad says he thinks the 18th Amendment will be repealed and that the Volstead Act will be annulled too. It's too bad, but I guess I have to agree with Dad that it didn't work very well. Human nature can't be changed, I suppose.

So glad to hear your flying goes well. Be sure and not write things so as to upset Mom, about the danger I mean. We want to hear all about it tho - well, you know what I mean.

Must grade papers. G'nite.
Myrtle

Randolph Field
Mar. 19, 1933

Folks,

This afternoon Ann Seale & mother had Ralph Read & I & a girl friend (& some others) of Ann's who has been going with Ralph over to Ann's birthday supper. Was splendid - turkey, etc., frozen custard & the cake. They called it my birthday cake too so we sort of had a double party. Much to the discomfiture of one Cadet Chuck Fischer, who is nuts over Ann & has been working hard to get her for 3 months. Old lady - not so old I guess - seems to sort of like me, I guess. We all had a lot of fun - all but Fischer.

Had an inspection yesterday, our first formal Saturday insp. since I was made Captain of A Company. Each of the 2 Captains inspects his own company and I really gave them a going over too. Probably the toughest they'll ever have. Good idea because from now on they'll be afraid to let down on a Saturday for they won't know when it will be duplicated.

Another of the boys, Rogers, crashed and was killed the other night. Were 6 of them on a night cross-country & the fog came in and forced them down. He got too low & flew into a hillside. Another boy flew blind above the fog from 9 until 12 midnight & finally had to join the Caterpillar Club ("hit the silk" that is) when he ran out of gas.

But don't worry about me. I always play safe - something looks bad I will jump - the heck with the airplane.

Bye - Orv

Randolph Field
May 9, 1933

Myrtle & Mom,

Had a letter out of a clear sky from Vivian Cyrus. She says, "Myrtle had the Jungle School kids write a community history and they gave it the day the Ladies Aid were there. It kept everyone absorbed the whole time. Why, MY name is even in the thing! She has surely done well at that school this year, everyone remarks about it."

Myrtle, I'm beginning to believe you're in a community only a little while until you're one of it's most outstanding bulwarks. I've heard fine comments from several sources on how well you did at the P.T.A. meeting at Tamarack, too.

Orv

Randolph Field
May 16, 1933

Folks,

Another X-Country tomorrow. We have been flying the Douglas BT almost exclusively. It's much bigger than the "A" Stage PT-3; has a 12 cylinder 400 H.P. Liberty motor.

This morning went out for a little dual went up to 12,000 feet. Cold as blazes up there but beautiful - nothing but blue sky above us & the glistening carpet of white below. The "Aviator's Halo" followed us about at Xpress train speed on the stratus clouds below. That is an phenomenon of the atmosphere known only to flyers. Your shadow on the clouds is surrounded by a complete rainbow of all colors. Sure pretty.

We spiraled down power off and Lt. George told me to try landing on a spot on the field. I came in, cut my gun at what I thought was the normal position, and it looked good to me. Then as I neared the spot I saw I was a little high so I slipped her down some more until it looked good and leveled off only to shoot across the spot 20 feet up. So I gave her the gun to go around again, expecting George to give me fits for as a rule Kimble & I (his students) are pretty hot. But when I looked around he was having a good laugh at my expense. After we landed he told me that my eyes weren't back to normal after differences in pressure from the high altitude where the eyeball lens becomes distorted. He said pursuit pilots that come down quick from high altitudes sometimes have to shoot at a field 4 or 5 times before they can hit it. The effect wears off in about 10 minutes.

Am fit as a fiddle. Don't worry about me.
Orvis

Randolph Field
June 1, 1933

Folks,

Had a little excitement today. After Ralph Read landed, his oleo landing strut broke off, dropping his wing and spinning him around. We lifted the ship up & put a saw horse under it. They put a new oleo member on though it will have to have the wing repaired as some of the ribs were broke.

Then my instructor took up Powers in the ship I had just vacated and went back over to Zeuhl Field for Powers to get a crack at the hurdles (the landings between the ropes I told you about). What does Powers do but come in & somehow drug his left wing and bounced over to his right. The landing gear collapsed & the ship slid along on her wing & nose, breaking both right wings & tying the prop in a knot. They brought it home in a truck.

Then over on A stage, dodo Wilson - who used to be a tenor soloist with Wayne King's Orchestra - had a propeller leave him. He made a safe landing.

But to cap the climax - Davis, a Kelly Field boy, took a pursuit ship out on transition. He was majoring in Bombardment and was used to flying those big old ships & had never flown a pea shooter before. The poor kid goes right over to where his girl friend lives out in the country and kills himself. He was doing a chandelle with her and her folks watching and he stalled & spun in. He practically committed suicide. Too bad but another lesson for the rest of us to keep the cobwebs out of the nut.

There was one funny thing that happened. Warner wanted me to take a Collier subscription he paid a beautiful girl agent $2.50 for. She hypnotized him into buying it. She bored into his eyes with hers until she had his name on the dotted line. When he got out of the storm, he didn't want the magazine. He will never hear the last of that. I took pity & told him I'd take it off his hands, and handed over the 2.50. I will send it to Aunt Mag.

I can tell you there is mighty little money in my pocket. When I left the pay line after taking care of PX, barber, tailor, laundry, insurance, and the school loan from Franklin College, you can see I was pretty light on my feet. The word is we will get full pay again after July 1st. Sure hope so.

Orvis

Randolph Field
June 8th, 1933

Folks,

We will be starting at Kelly Field very shortly but I still don't know what to take there. If we would get permanent regular commissions (like the West Point boys here already have) than Observation would be my choice. But truth be known reserve commissions seem to be the only thing in the cards for us Cadets. I don't want Attack, for they'd stick me down here at Fort Crockett & goodness knows I don't want to stay in Texas more than a year. Bombardment gives one time on big multi-motored ships & you know I've always liked the big airplanes. Guess will have to let the powers that be decide, tho if you are high up in your class (which I am) they pretty much give you what you ask for.

Orv

Randolph Field
June 23, 1933

Folks,

Well, after eight months of concentrated everything our training at Randolph is finished. Only 43 out of the original 124 Cadets who started are left. I took my final check ride with my flight commander & received one of the scant compliments ever handed out around here when he told me, after we landed, that "That was a very good ride."

"Stormy Weather" playing again on the radio. Never seem to get tired of it.

When we go across town we start in all over again, this time in the biggest ships in the Army - the Keystone and Martin Two-Engine Bombers. That should be easy, as we are supposed to be finished Flyers now, as far as flying itself is concerned. Have to learn the fine points of flying bombers & the mission connected therewith. They also will make us "officers & gentlemen" through instruction in military knowledge, discipline, and the social graces.

Orv

P.S. In less than 10 days I'll be a Kelly Field Mister!

Kelly Field
San Antonio, Texas
July 21, 1933

Folks,

Don't believe I mentioned in my last letter I was made Flying Cadet Captain of the Cadet Detachment. Considering the caliber of boys here, this is the highest honor I have ever been paid.

Monday we start "blind flying," where you fly entirely from instruments. They have the PT-3's fixed up with the rear cockpit hooded over so that all you can see is your bank and turn, rate of climb & air speed indicators, tachometer and compass. The idea is to fly through fog safely if we ever get caught out.

Been doing a lot of formation flying & bombing practice. Start out with the familiar 3 plane V & then go to the 6-9-12 ship formations. We fly in teams; Baldwin flies the airplane for me while I act as bombardier, and then vice versa. The Keystone's have a top speed of only 15 m.p.h. above a stall so it requires a lot of brute strength to fly the things.

Knocked off my 200th hour today. Enough for a transport license in civilian aviation. Another hundred to go here at Kelly.

I'm enclosing a few snaps. The part of the bomber that you can see behind me doesn't show

Orvis with unidentified guests. This two-engine Keystone bomber represented World War One technology and was already obsolete in 1933.

The Kelly Field Mister.

Due to their under-powered engines, unclean lines, and high drag, these ships were barely able to maintain a safe cruising speed.

it's size but maybe you can grasp the significance when you realize that a person can walk standing up under the bottom wing - it's 17 feet to the top wing. You can see the rip cord on my parachute by my left hand.

Dad wrote Myrtle will teach at Bell Horn Bay school this year. That's great - she can walk to school from her cabin.

Bye - Orv

Kelly Field
Sept 10, 1933

Mom,

Had an interesting experience. Was doing a high speed taxi - rolling along about 50 m.p.h. - when the ship just fell on one wing and skidded on her nose into a ground loop. I had cut the switches as the ship went up so the propellers were not injured, but the rest of it was pretty badly damaged. Crew chief came running up to me, breathless, asking if I was all right. I said, "Yes, I'm all right," but when I got out I had to lean against the fuselage because my legs were so rubbery. Turns out we found a break in the rear strut, part of which was old and rusted.

One of the Observation boys, Robert Scott, had a crash when dragging a strange field at night. He was low on fuel & needed to get down quickly. He did not see a high tension line and, knowing he could not go over it, sailed below the wires. As luck would have it, just at that moment his motor died from lack of fuel and he went in on rough ground. He climbed out of the wreck & looked in disgust at the level-as-a-floor three hundred acre field just behind him!

Awful glad Carr has agreed to drive you down to my graduation, Mom. It's definitely Oct 14th, so plan accordingly. I've been told unofficially that I will be assigned to the 11th Bombardment Squadron at March Field, Riverside, California. They use the big 12-ton two-motored Curtiss Condor Bombers. I've bought a car, so we will take it to the West Coast & Dennis can drive yours home afterward. I think it better all the way round if you keep house for me over the winter & return to Sandy in the spring or summer - let things with you and Dad simmer down awhile.

Orv

Chippewa Falls, Wisc.
Sept 15th, 1933

Myrtle,

Charlie and I will be able to stay with you for the winter while your Mother is in Calif. with Orvis. I will go up to Sandy when she leaves, & Myrtle, you and I will batch it until Charlie comes up.

I have a few preserves, pickles, and a little sauce to start out with - probably 4 or 5 jars of food, so that will be something. You surely will have to be my side kick if I come up alone; I'm afraid to stay alone nights, so there - you can't desert me anytime.

Nice that you can be with Orvis, Mrs. Nelson. As you said it is hard for you to have your family so far apart. I'll take good care of Myrtle - you won't have to worry. Surely hope Mr. Nelson will be able to make a go of it this time. I can understand it is not easy in business, especially in these times.

Gert Hughes

Kelly Field
Oct 15-33

Marcus,

What a glorious day yesterday was! I am so happy I was here to see it esp. after I lost out on his college graduation. They started out with a Flying Review, was 85 ships that took part. Every boy flew his ship low over the Field, where we & all the big shots stood. Carr had tears in his eyes, me too.

Then after the boys all landed, we went to the Post Theater. Prayers were given by the Chaplain of Kelly Field, then Colonel Martin, Commandant of Randolph Field, made the Graduation Address and General Danforth presented them their diplomas, commissions as Reserve Second Lieutenants, and what Orvis calls "our cherished objective" -- the Silver Wings of the Army Air Corps.

I have the newspaper clippings & programs. Will keep & show them to you when get home. Was 39 Regular officers from West Point (they had already been commissioned) and 46 Cadets (like Orvis). Some company our son is running in am so proud of him.

Orvis wants to sightsee as much as we can as neither of us have seen New Mexico or Arizona. I hope to get some sketching done, for to paint during this winter.

Mamie

The Air Corps Advanced Flying School requests the honor of your presence at the Graduation Exercises at Kelly Field, Texas, October 14, 1933.

Aerial Review 8:00 A.M.

Exercises Post Theatre 10:00 A.M.

Grand Canyon Nat'l Park
Oct 30-33

Myrtle, Gert, Marcus, and all inquiring friends,

Yesterday Orvis & I rode on mule back down Bright Angel Trail to bottom of Grand Canyon. Cost 6.00 each. And was it some ride. I'd not missed if for the world but I was so tired coming out and sore. I just about laid on the saddle. It was a day trip, ate lunch next to Colorado River. Orvis got cold, had left his big coat behind as we were in a hurry. I seem to have forgotten my old ways of always carrying too many wraps.

You cannot realize a ride like this on a narrow zig-zag trail, unless you take it or one like it. Sometimes, I could look boldly down below and beyond, but most time I felt sick in the pit of my stomach and was glad to try to show nonchalance by being very much interested in the formation of the steep rockwall at my side. My mule was very fond of stopping at a turn and gazing out wistfully with her head and neck out over infinity, as Orvis called it. They are sure nerveless animals. We think it's one mile down from the rim. I slept in late this morning from the effects.

Went thro Carlsbad Cave, petrified forest, cliff dweller ruins, Painted Desert, much more. Enclosed black & white cards do not do justice.

Mom

WINS WINGS—Lieut. Orvis Nelson, former Franklin College student and for three years a member of the Baptists' football squad, was recently given a commission in the Air Corps Reserve upon graduation from the Army's advanced flying school at Kelly Field, San Antonio, Tex., and is now on active duty at March Field, Riverside, Cal.

Tingdale Bros.
November 10, 1933

Marcus:

I have your letter and note what you say about the obligations to the First National Bank. We have nothing at all to pay the bank now; people are not paying us, and this is tax time so the comparatively few who are still holding their property are paying on taxes. People are dropping property right and left regardless of how much they have paid in. Now we can get the property back but, of course, that is of

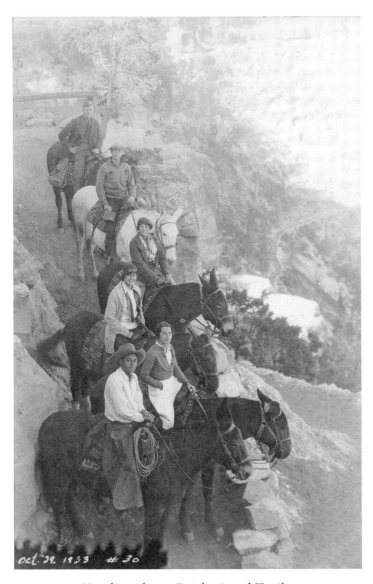

Heading down Bright Angel Trail.
Orvis at top, Mamie third from top.

to get anything you owe us. I know that you are not in a position to pay, and what would I gain to give it to an attorney? We are in exactly the same position.

If you have not yet closed with Mr. Fred Groth on our lands, please return all quit claim deeds & paper to us, and do not cut any timber off our lands or let Mr. Groth cut any, because we have got some hard deals on it and we can no longer wait on him to act on the original deal. We have got to move fast, sell if off forty by forty, and show some green in the till immediately.

Martin

P.S. For your information, Rudolph is sick in bed and I am working fifteen hours a day and cannot do everything without having to delegate some of the work. When I ask someone in the office to write a letter for me it is just exactly the same as if I dictated it myself.

Riverside, California
Nov 13-33

Girlie

Rec. your two letters & card of Thurs. I was worried about not hearing but Orvis said I need not worry but I can't help it since you and Orvis are so much to me.

O. took me around the Field this morning to look at all the planes. His 11th Bombardment Squadron insignia is funny, they put one on side of every plane. Color figure of cartoon character Jiggs with cigar in mouth, cane in one hand and bomb under other arm. ha.

I washed today. We hire the worst of it but it costs so much so I do what is not tiring. Yesterday, I waxed floors and baked bread. Orvis says I do too much but I wish to earn my keep.

Did you and Gert mulch my roses? Hope you did but if snow interferes then do it in spring when it melts. Hope you did it as freezing & thawing hurts them.

Orvis has had only 2 flights, short ones. Seems Gov't hasn't much money so flights are spaced out. He gets lonesome to fly. He is quite impressed with his Commanding Officer, Lt. Col. H.H. Arnold. Men call him "Hap", but not to his face.

Mom

P.S. O. got word the pilots are to get a 15% cut in pay & flying time limited even more. Not happy.

no avail. It helps no one. We are, therefore, carrying everyone along as much as we can.

Leniency, especially by the banks, has been asked by President Roosevelt, so I do not think that the Banking Department will make a very drastic demand on the Aitkin First National Bank on account of our note. However, that may be all words because everybody is hounding us strongly enough.

If our creditors do not wish to be patient and let us work things out, there is nothing left here. Unless something happens in Washington soon to change the monetary system so that the ten million Americans who are out of work can get work, almost every institution is sunk and the result will be chaos.

You see, Marcus, nearly all our customers are in the same shape as you are and as we are. For instance, what good would it be for us to threaten you for specific performance of your contracts or try

Thanksgiving Day, 1933 at Riverside, Calif.

Tingdale Bros.
November 20, 1933

Marcus:

Will you please without delay return the Quit Claim Deeds on the Groth lands. We cannot wait any longer.

You say "forget the Aitkin garage." You know I am very anxious to pay on the First National note. Of course I am like you, "independently poor," to use your own words. We have less than nothing left, but I would like to see Hassman paid out. Could we not rent out the garage and turn the money over to him?

Business is poorer than ever, Minneapolis seems to be at a stand-still. Perhaps that is not strange owing to the fact that the crops of the Northwest were more or less lost, and instead of the farmers having money to give to the cities, most of them will be on charity this winter.

Have you any way of getting a truck-load of wood, any kind would do, mixed or otherwise; that is, if it can be done without any cash outlay, for that we have none.

Martin

P.S. Run right over to the post office this very minute and mail me those deeds.

Riverside
Dec 14-33

Sister Deocia,

I notice I have three dresses I have not used so much but are a little tight for me so I will try to send to you can use in your family some way I guess.

I took Orvis down a little last night at supper for never giving thanks at meals. I had taught my children to say grace when small but their father's unsympathetic attitude toward religion has gotten them out of it. I know Myrtle is same. I should like to warn young folks to marry believers, for many reasons.

I feel kind of worried about Myrtle. She is all in so her housekeeper writes me. She works too hard on extra school programs. Gert said she puts Myrtle to bed after supper now so she gets rested to keep going. She always takes too much responsibility in school affairs.

Marcus writes he is much better but gets lonesome. He gets sick so easy.

Orvis is flying a little and goes to school one day a week. Army has sent most of ships to P.I. and Hawaii, so until new ones come they will not get much flying. He made a parachute jump the other day. Last boy out broke his leg. Orvis has been up about 3 miles he says it's terrible cold up there in an open cockpit.

Mamie

P.S. Forgot to say I have enrolled in the Artist Club in Riverside.

In 1936, Mamie (third from left) also managed six weeks at the Art School at Plymouth, Mass. It was here she "took knife work."

Jack Be Nimble

Say the rhyme "Jack Be
Nimble":
    Jack be nimble
    Jack be quick
    Jack jump over the candle-
       stick.
Do the action inferred.
For variation Jack might hop,
  skip, or run over the candlestick.

Little Sally Ann

"Little Sally Ann
Sitting in the sand
A weeping and a wailing
For a nice young man,
Arise, Sally, arise
And wipe your dirty eyes
Turn to the east
and turn to the west
And turn to the very one
That you love best!"

Jacob + Rachel

    Players form a circle. One person
is chosen for Jacob and one for Rachel.
Jacob is blind-folded. He calls "Rachel,
where are you?" She answers "Here I
am", trying to disguise her voice. The
object is for Jacob to tag Rachel.

Your Toes, Your Knees, Your Shoulders, Your Head

Sing:
  Your toes, your knees, your
  shoulders, your head
Three times and point to
each part of your body.
Sing:- And clap our hands
    together-
Tune:- Mulberry Bush

Run Dodge Ball

There are two teams. One team
forms a circle and the other
team stands inside. The players
in the circle try to hit those
in the center with the ball.
As soon as a person is hit
he is out.

Leap Frog and Forward Roll

Teams line up behind mat.
First person stoops on end of mat.
Second person leaps over first, does
a forward roll, coming back in place.
When all are finished, they do a
forward roll all together.

Myrtle kept hundreds of 3x5 inch cards describing various children's games, poems, exercises, and nutrition.

WAR DEPARTMENT THEATRE

MARCH FIELD RIVERSIDE, CALIFORNIA

1934 APRIL 1934

SUNDAY	MONDAY	TUESDAY	WEDNESDAY	THURSDAY	FRIDAY	SATURDAY
1	2 — I AM SUZANNE / LILIAN HARVEY / GENE RAYMOND; PATHE NEWS	3 — CHANCE AT HEAVEN / GINGER ROGERS / JOEL MC CREA; SCREEN SOUVENIR / WHERE'S THAT TIGER / PATHE NEWS	4 — EIGHT GIRLS IN A BOAT / DOROTHY WILSON / DOUGLAS MONTGOMERY; EDDIE DUCHIN & BAND / GOOFYTONE NEWS	5 — HIPS HIPS HOORAY / WHEELER & WOOLSEY / RUTH ETTING; STRANGE AS IT SEEMS / ALLEZ OOP / FOX NEWS	6 — THE LAST ROUNDUP / RANDOLPH SCOTT / BARBARA FRITCHIE; INTO THE DEPTHS / SCREEN SNAPSHOT / FOX NEWS	7 — SIX OF A KIND / CHARLES RUGGLES / MARY BOLAND; KISSING TIME / GEM OF THE SEA / RADIO ROUNDUP
8	9 — EASY TO LOVE / GENEVIEVE TOBIN / ADOLPH MENJOU; AIR TONIC / PETTING IN THE PARK / PATHE NEWS	10 — WHITE WOMAN / CAROLE LOMBARD / CHAS. LAUGHTON; BARGAIN OF THE CENTURY / PATHE NEWS	11 — I LIKE IT THAT WAY / GLORIA STUART / GEO. PRYOR; SUITS TO NUTS / PARKING SPACE / THROTTLE PUSHERS	12 — ALL OF ME / FREDRIC MARCH / MARIAN HOPKINS; HARMONICA RASCALS / SCREEN SOUVENIR / FOX NEWS	13 — SMOKY / VICTOR JORY / IRENE BENTLEY; FLIP'S LUNCHROOM / DEATH CRASH / FOX NEWS	14 — MISS FANE'S BABY IS STOLEN / DOROTHEA WIECK / ALICE BRADY; MEET THE CHAMP / GOOFYTONE NEWS
15	16 — BOLERO / GEORGE RAFT / CAROLE LOMBARD; THE RIOT CALL / LIKE THE BIRDIES SING / PATHE NEWS	17 — GOING HOLLYWOOD / MARION DAVIES / BING CROSBY; CITY OF WAX / WHAT PRICE SPEED / PATHE NEWS	18 — FOG / DONALD COOK / MARY BRIAN; NOT TONIGHT JOSEPHINE / TUNE DETECTIVE	19 — AS HUSBANDS GO / WARNER BAXTER / HELEN VINSON; SCREEN SOUVENIR / FOX NEWS	20 — STRAIGHTAWAY / TIM MC COY / SUE CAROL; FORGOTTEN BABIES / CHASING DOOM / FOX NEWS	21 — SON OF THE DESERT / LAUREL & HARDY / DOROTHY CHRISTIE; PICTURE PALACE / SCRAPING THE SKY / STRANGE AS IT SEEMS
22	23 — LOST PATROL / VICTOR MC LAGLEN / BORIS KARLOFF; JACK DENNY AND BAND / HONEYMOON HOTEL / PATHE NEWS	24 — BY CANDLELIGHT / PAUL LUCAS / ELISSA LANDI; SLOW POKE / STOOPNOCRACY / PATHE NEWS	25 — FASHION OF 1934 / WILLIAM POWELL / BETTE DAVIS; CHINA SHOP / MOSCOW / FAST FINGERS	26 — MAN OF TWO WORLDS / FRANCIS LEDERER / ELISSA LANDI; FOX NEWS	27 — FRONTIER MARSHAL / GEORGE O'BRIEN / IRENE BENTLEY; THE LION TAMER / FOX NEWS	28 — HI NELLIE / PAUL MUNI / GLENDA FARRELL; VAUDEVILLE ON PARADE
29	30 — GOOD DAME / SYLVIA SIDNEY / FREDRIC MARCH; SCREEN SOUVENIR / THE OLD MAN OF THE MOUNTAIN / PATHE NEWS					

0 - FAMILY AUDIENCE 00 - MATURE AUDIENCE

Bell Horn Bay School
Sandy Lake
January 22, 1934

Miss Nelson,

It is too bad you are so sick, but we are sure you will get well soon and be back with us again.

Wally was fishing most of the time over the weekend but only got fifteen crappies. He and Lyman went spearing and hit a fifteen pounder in the tail but didn't get it.

We have to drink out of a jar with a faucet on it. Mr. Halich has to carry water from the fire tower.

Yours truly,
Arnold Koerber
Wallace & Clifford Ekelund

Tingdale Bros.
Jan 25 - 1934

Marcus,

Yes, I will send you a pair of snowshoes. Will you return them as soon as you are through.

This is confidential so keep it to yourself. It should not be discussed with anyone -

"I know a man with heart trouble & hardening of the arteries. He started to drink Bulgarian Buttermilk, and got well. He took it 3 times a day. If a person can refrain from salt, pepper, coffee, tea, and meats, eggs, and fish, the cure is much surer."

The Bulgarians live to 100 because their milk keeps the arteries soft and that is all there is to it. Don't tell anybody. We do not want anyone to laugh at us. Try it in secret and if it fails, no one will scoff.

BUT IT WILL MAKE A NEW MAN OF YOU!
Martin

Riverside
Feb 1, 1934

Dad & Myrtle,

Just time to dash off a card. Several of us took our Written & Flight Tests for the Department of Commerce Air Transport License today. Took it in a Curtiss Condor. Nice to have.

Little flying - lots of sitting around.
Orv

Rockwell Field San Diego, Calif.
March 6, 1934

Loading the Salt Lake City to Seattle air mail. The men are armed.

Dad & Myrtle,

Things are nothing but a blur here. You probably read in the papers that on February 9th President Roosevelt decided to cancel all the airmail contracts with the air lines, and turn them over to the Army.

Well, Lt. Col. Arnold was appointed Commander of the Western Operations of the Army Mail & immediately got things started. He had all the Condors lined up on March Field with their destinations chalked on the sides. We took off immediately to establish terminals at every important station between Cheyenne, Wyo. and the Coast.

I was assigned to go to Cheyenne to see to getting things set up there, over a thousand miles of mountain country. As usual, I took along my crew chief, that dour old Scot, Sgt. McPheeters. We refueled at Las Vegas and expected to make Salt Lake City by dark. Despite our heavy flying suits, the Sgt. and I sat hunched up in the cockpit with twenty degree below zero winds whistling around us. We were late getting out of Las Vegas because we couldn't get one engine started so we were alone - rest of the boys had gone on ahead. I had been flying for some time, over unknown terrain, when I begun to be uncertain of my position. I asked McPheeters to get the map out. His hands were numb with cold and he lost his grip when a gust of wind caught the map. That shook me. I had no radio to tune in a range - I was dependent totally on my maps and dead reckoning. Frantic, I looked toward the rear of the airplane and, to my surprise, saw the map had lodged several feet behind the cockpit near a strut. It was fluttering madly in the wind.

I said, "We've got to get that map Sergeant. You fly and I'll crawl out and get it." But after 30 seconds of him behind the wheel I realized that would never do. I said, "You'll have to go." He looked at me, then the map, then back at me. With tears running down his cheeks from the cold, he took off his

parachute so the wind wouldn't blow it open, and creeped out of the cockpit. Slowly he inched his way back and reached out his hand with a slow motion movement that made me hold my breath. Somehow he grabbed hold of it and got back, and boy that was a relief. I soon located our position.

After checking in at Cheyenne we settled down with some of the boys only to hear the radio calmly announce the deaths of Lieutenants Grenier and White, who crashed ten minutes out of Salt Lake. Then the announcer went on to tell us that Eastham was dead after hitting a tree attempting to land at Jerome, Idaho. We all silently went to our quarters.

By the time I got back to March Field a couple of days later, a dozen boys had been killed or injured and we had hardly even gotten into business. Colonel Arnold knew what was happening instantly - the Army was sublimely ignorant of actual weather flying. He assigned 18 of us to depart immediately for Rockwell Field to learn "blind" flying.

That was nearly two weeks ago, and we are almost through the crash course. Lots of ground school, plus practice flying "under the hood." I feel now I can handle the plane blind in any maneuver and recover from stalls & spins easily. Also, have had a lot of radio beam navigation training. You listen to the Morse code signals transmitting from the station and you can tell by what comes in whether you are flying to or from a station and which of the four quadrants (east, west, north, south) you are in.

Expect orders any day to return to March and get a mail assignment. I am looking forward to it.

Orv

March Field
March 10, 1934

Dad & Myrtle,

Am to leave tomorrow to fly the night mail out of Reno. We will be using Douglas B-7 Bombers - a high winged monoplane with two 750 H.P. Conqueror engines, plus a hand cranked retractable landing gear. Pretty fast - it cruises at 150 m.p.h. Unfortunately, it has a high landing speed as well, 80-90 m.p.h.; compared to the 50-60 of a Keystone or Condor. Makes it tricky if you think how fast that really is when you make contact with the ground.

Mom is going to come out to Reno in a couple of days to stay with me. I'll have a regular schedule; leave Reno for Oakland at 2:00 A.M. and then return to Reno at 9:00 P.M. They call it the "grave yard shift." Nice name, huh?

Orv

March Field
March 29, 1934

Dad & Myrtle,

I was ordered back here yesterday. Mom will follow me in a few days. She sure has been a good soldier & a real help to me. Every night she met me when I landed back at Reno. But it was getting hard on her sleep and one night I was delayed and didn't get in til 3 A.M. There was a note on my car that she had decided to go home & get some sleep. I kidded her unmercifully for finally having given up waiting to see me crash.

One thing has been found out, that got so many of the boys killed early on. When flying in the mountains from one light beacon to the next, while the pilot could make the next beacon out ahead, he sometimes could not see to the one beyond, due to worsening visibility. That usually meant he could no longer see the one behind him either. As he was trained, he would set up an orbit around the one beacon he could see, and wait for a break in the weather. But, as he flew around that one light in the dark, with no other reference, his orbit became more & more elliptical; with each revolution he would slowly dip closer and closer to the ground until finally crashing.

I expect I will get another mail assignment in a week or so. Army doesn't want us to forget our regular jobs but right now they have us running around doing fool things instead of flying. Congress does not give the Air Corps enough money to operate properly.

Orv

Tingdale Bros.
June 1st - 1934

Marcus,

I am glad to know you are finally going after that State House seat. You have had your eye on it for some time, so happy action has been taken.

I like your platform. Why not use as a slogan this thought:

"Do Not Tax Mother Earth,
Tax The Earnings Made From It."

I hope we may elect all representatives, senators, and governor, who believe like you do. Gov. Olson is against a gross earnings tax. It is the only honest tax too.

Martin

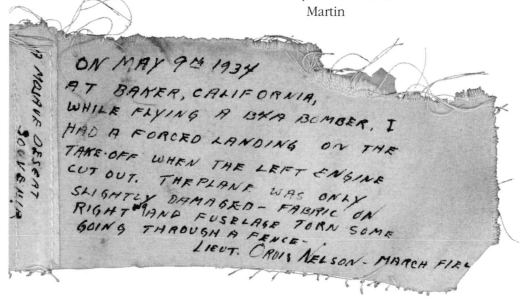

ON MAY 9TH 1934 AT BAKER, CALIFORNIA, WHILE FLYING A B7A BOMBER, I HAD A FORCED LANDING ON THE TAKE-OFF WHEN THE LEFT ENGINE CUT OUT. THE PLANE WAS ONLY SLIGHTLY DAMAGED - FABRIC ON RIGHT HAND FUSELAGE TORN SOME GOING THROUGH A FENCE -
LIEUT. ORVIS NELSON - MARCH FIEL[D]

IN MOJAVE DESERT SOUVENIR

Actual fabric from the aircraft

East Lake, Minn.
June 2, 1934

Marcus,

    In answer to your question, it is my understanding the Works Progress Administration will soon begin building concrete sidewalks, curbs, and put down a paved road through the main street of Tamarack. If you so desire, you may pass this information along to your prospective constituents.
    Carl Magnuson
    4th District County Commissioner

AITKIN REPUBLICAN
September 7, 1934

SANDY LAKE NEWS -
Last Sunday Marcus & Mamie Nelson hosted an "old settlers" picnic at their place on Prairie River. About 100 people attended. They were the perfect hosts and said they wanted to make it a yearly observance.

Mr. Nelson's Platform

TO THE VOTERS OF AITKIN COUNTY:

    Having entered the Primary Election race as a candidate for Representative from Aitkin County, I feel that I should present a definite plan for getting the relief we need if Aitkin County is to survive.

    About 70% of the taxes of Aitkin County were delinquent; on January 1, 1934, we had $3,414,123 in uncollected taxes. We cannot continue the old system of taxation.

    If nominated and elected to represent the people of Aitkin County, I will work and vote for the following laws:

1. Gross Income tax as replacement tax only.
2. Exemption of all taxes on homes and farms.
3. Exemption of personal property tax.
4. Authority for County Boards to make tax settlements on the installment plan on farms and homes occupied by the owner.
5. Authority for counties to take over delinquent lands suitable for agriculture, and the right to sell same, paying out of the proceeds all public debt on lands affected. All other receipts to go into a general fund to be used where most needed. Land not suitable for farming to go to the state.
6. Wild land tax on lands not used for home or farming on a basis so low that people holding land for future homes or for an investment will pay their taxes.
7. Authorize county, villages, towns, and school districts to issue refunding bonds, to buy bonds, or certificates of outstanding indebtedness, at a discount, in order to get their business on a cash basis.
8. Give part of the gas tax to township roads for building and maintenance.
9. Give county the right to salvage dead and down timber and sell hay stumpage on unoccupied delinquent land, where it is liable to go to waste—crediting same on taxes of the land affected.
10. A member from the county on the state conservation committee to take part in all matters pertaining to lands in the county affected.

    There are several other counties in the state with problems the same as ours. If elected I will get in touch with their representatives and try to induce them to work together in order to get the necessary relief.

    Thanking you for whatever support you feel you can give me, I am,
    Yours truly,
    MARCUS NELSON

Issued by Marcus Nelson, McGregor, Minn.

MINNESOTA EDUCATION ASSOCIATION
Northern Division
Warroad, Minnesota
Sept. 24, 1934

Miss Nelson:

    May we have your support in the cause of protecting the public school teaching profession by again becoming a member of the Minnesota Education Association? This organization is doing more to protect your job and your school than any other organization.

    If you are an experienced teacher of several years, undoubtedly your salary has been reduced. Further reductions may be looked for unless tax burdens can be more fairly distributed. This association is doing everything it can to that end, but we must still see it through.

    The M.E.A. has exercised influence in the past with our legislature. Four years ago it got an adequate teachers' retirement act passed. But more must be done and everyone must do their share.

    Won't you send in your two dollars today?
    P.W. Chase
    Pres. No. Division
Addition by Miss Millard:
    I wish that we might make Aitkin County one of the counties of the state which have a one hundred per cent enrollment in the M.E.A. Let us all work toward that goal.
    Harriet Millard
    Aitkin Co. Supt. of Schools

AITKIN REPUBLICAN
November 1, 1934

SANDY LAKE NEWS -
Myrtle Nelson and Runar Pasell, popular Bill Horn Bay teachers, expect to present their much-in-demand puppet show, "The Three Pigs," at Lawler on Fri. evening, November 9th.

NOTICE OF NOMINATION

OF

CANDIDATE WITHOUT PARTY DESIGNATION

Aitkin _____ County, Minn.

COUNTY AUDITOR'S OFFICE _June 23rd_ 1934

To _Marcus Nelson_ _____ and All Whom It May Concern:

Pursuant to the provisions of the General Election Laws you are hereby notified of your nomination as a candidate without party designation for the office of State Legislature

_____ _at a Primary Election held on the eighteenth day of June, 1934._
Your name will therefore be placed on the Election Ballot for said office at the ensuing General Election.

County Auditor.

NOTE:—When only two persons file for an office without party designation, or not more than twice the number of persons to be elected to any Non-Partisan office, file for nomination thereof, their names shall not be placed on the Primary Election Ballot, without party designation but said persons shall be considered and shall be the nominees for such office and their names shall be placed on the General Election Ballots as such nominees.

AITKIN REPUBLICAN
November 8, 1934

LOCAL ITEMS -
Marcus Nelson, who last Tuesday defeated incumbent 54th District Representative G.W. Alfs by 3,678 votes to 2,430 votes, was in town yesterday thanking voters for their support. He informs us that Mrs. Nelson has gone to Hamilton Field, Calif. to visit their son, Lieut. Orvis M. Nelson, a bomber pilot recently assigned to that location.

AITKIN REPUBLICAN
December 13, 1934

SANDY LAKE NEWS -
Myrtle Nelson, daughter of Representative-elect Marcus Nelson, and Runar Pasell gave yet another outstanding puppet show performance in Brainerd last week. "The Big Bad Wolf" was very popular with both young and old alike. The acting and dancing dolls brought almost continuous howls of glee from even the most crusty spectator. They expect to keep doing their shows for as long as people enjoy them, which from the look of things, could be a good while indeed.

Nelson's Camp
12/23/34

C/O Orvis Nelson, Hamilton Field
    San Rafael, Calif.
Wife:
    Your xmas card rec'd, also letter.
    Things are quiet here - crew gone. I have been alone for 2 days. Am going to Aitkin tomorrow to get my picture taken for Roger's Gallery in St. Paul. Myrtle & I to take xmas dinner at Martin & Hazel Sorensen's.
    Orvis how do you like your new digs up San Francisco way? I would like to hear what you think of that country.
    Marcus

Myrtle's Puppet Theater

An original production by Myrtle and Runar. They built this puppet stage.

The Three Little Pigs.

MISS NELSON RECOGNIZED AUTHORITY ON MARIONETTES

Special to The Republican

By Shamrock
Correspondent

Miss Myrtle Nelson, who recently returned from an extensive air tour of the U. S. and Canada, has been requested to exhibit her popular marionette theater at the Duluth State Teachers' College. She went on Tuesday with a group of her pupils to present "The Three Little Pigs" at the educational institution. Miss Nelson also gave a talk on marionette and puppet shows. She is the daughter of Representative and Mrs. Marcus Nelson.

*February 20, 1936 edition of
the Aitkin Republican.*

Hamilton Field
December 31, 1934

Dad,

We are flying the new Martin B-10 Bomber, a two engine monoplane. Has retractable gear, enclosed cockpit, and fine, clean lines - very fast. This is the best new ship the Army has gotten in a long time. With this we can now hold our own with the Boeing 247, the civilian airline transport. We sure have taken a lot of ribbing from the airline boys about their ships being faster than ours.

With the lack of appropriations from Congress I don't know how much longer my active duty will be extended. Will have to hang on for now, because this time of year it is almost impossible to hook up with an airline.

Mom sends her best.

Orv

BARNEY FINNEGAN
Fifty-second District

THEO. THIELEN
Fifty-third District

WM. A. SYREEN
Fifty-third District

WILLIAM H. HALL
Fifty-third District

MARCUS NELSON
Fifty-fourth District

Marcus' official portrait in the 1935 Minnesota Legislative Manual.

Aitkin County Board
January 5th, 1935

Honorable Marcus Nelson:

We offer our congratulations on your new responsibility and our hopes toward an improved future.

We, again, want to take up the matter of the tremendous amount of county debt and it's long range effect, owing to the difficult economic times in our county and our current system of taxation.

Marcus, you must make clear to those people down there our difficulty. Some of our taxing units are bankrupt or very near so. A very considerable part of this debt, especially school debt, are loans from the State Trust Funds where the levies are arbitrarily made on a basis of what was collected during the past year. This brings the levies up to a point where it is absolutely impossible for anyone to pay taxes on any honest valuation. The net result is that the loans are in default and not anywhere near the tax revenue is collected to operate either the schools or the other local activities.

Martin B-10 bombers at Hamilton Field, just north of San Francisco.

WE DO NOT WANT CHARITY: GIVE US LEGISLATION THAT WILL GIVE US A CHANCE TO WORK OUT OUR OWN SALVATION.

NEITHER DO WE WANT OUR IDENTITY AS A LOCAL GOVERNMENTAL UNIT DESTROYED BY BEING ABSORBED AND GOVERNED BY A BUREAU OR DEPT LOCATED IN SOME MARBLE PALACE IN WASHINGTON OR ST. PAUL.

Sincerely,
The Aitkin Board of Commissioners

Journal of the House
FORTY-NINTH SESSION
First Day
St. Paul, Tuesday, January 8, 1935

In accordance with the Constitution and laws of the State of Minnesota, the members of the House of Representatives assembled in the Hall of Representatives in the Capitol in St. Paul on Tuesday, the Eighth day of January, A.D. 1935.

At the hour of 12 o'clock noon Hon. Mike Holm, Secretary of State, proceeded to call the body to order and designated Hon. Harry L. Wahlstrand, twenty-fifth District Representative, as Clerk pro tempore.

Prayer by Rev. C.H. Hook.

The Secretary of State then proceeded to call the several representative districts in numerical order and the one hundred thirty-one members-elect from said districts arose and the oath of office was administered by the Hon. Andrew Holt, Associate Justice of the Supreme Court of the State of Minnesota.

The Clerk then called the roll and a quorum was present.

The House then proceeded to the election of a Speaker.

Mr. George W. Johnson, Duluth, was placed in nomination and seconded.

Mr. Harold H. Barker, Elbow Lake, was placed in nomination and seconded.

The question being taken on the election of a Speaker, the roll was called.

Mr. Johnson received 82 votes.

Mr. Barker received 49 votes.

Mr. Johnson, having received the votes of a majority of all the members, was declared duly elected Speaker of the House.

Thereupon the members set themselves about the business of the people.

At 3:55 P.M., Mr. Brophy moved that the House do now adjourn.

Which motion prevailed.

And the Speaker declared the House adjourned until 10 A.M. tomorrow.

John I. Levin
Chief Clerk, House of
Representatives

Minnesota State Capitol in St. Paul, as it looked in 1920.

State Of Minnesota
HOUSE OF REPRESENTATIVES
Saint Paul
January 9th, 1935

Honorable Marcus Nelson
Ryan Hotel
Sir:

I have the honor of informing you that your salary as State Representative has been set at $1,000.00 per annum.

On this day, Hon. John M. Zwach, 14th District, Chairman of the Committee on Mileage moved his report and it was adopted by the House. Your expense voucher will be drawn up as follows: 328 miles at 6.667 cents per mile = $21.87

John I. Levin
Chief Clerk, House of Representatives

San Rafael
Sun, Jan 20-35

Husband,

Orvis and I after church & dinner sat around & talked up an idea to have a Historical Pageant at Sandy Lake. Charge admittance. The point at mouth of Prairie River be a good place, using water as well as land. Can also seat people on Anderson's bluff across the river. Canoes and bateau's come down Prairie River just as in olden times. Get Indians in birch bark canoes, make conical homes out of birch bark, which are to remain from year to year. Have their handmade goods on display.

Will have to hunt up facts of history of the Sandy Lake region. Indian period, time of French voyageurs and trappers, coming of white man.

Should be interesting to have one scene of an Indian marriage ceremony. Main character being Elsie Borg for bride and Myrtle for groom, as she likes to act as man from former years. Have war dances too. Maurice Nelson should be one actor - be a swell clown. Hazel Sorensen as master of ceremonies. Dad, you to look after the crowd & helpers. Need one person to take in money. Small charge first year but as it was enlarged more of a charge can be made. Whatever left over to be divided among the main drag. ha. ha.

The play would be more realistic on account of the water and the farther shores for use of the voyageurs and Indians and pioneers. Indians could even have a native Indian funeral if they not object. Take very little clearing to fix the point up.

Dad, would you not take great delight in it? Also it would make ad for your planned expansion of fishing camp. Tell us what you think.

Mamie

AITKIN REPUBLICAN
January 24, 1935

MARCUS NELSON ON SIX COMMITTEES

Representative Nelson has won appointments on six of the most important committees of the House. He will participate on drainage, game and fish, public domain, reforestation, taxes and tax laws, and towns and counties legislation. Mr. Nelson stated he would be sending along information relative to several bills he plans to introduce, so that constituents at home will have first hand data as to what the local solon hopes to get through for their benefit. Aitkinites who have been at the Capitol report that Mr. Nelson is already one of the best-known and best-liked members of the House. When he appears with Former Sheriff Carl Lind, who is a committee clerk in the legislature, the two make quite an impression on St. Paul streets as "men from Paul Bunyan's country."

An Analysis of the Omnibus Tax Relief Program and What It Will Do to Cut Taxes of Minnesota Farmers
By: Minnesota Federation of Associations for Tax Reform
February, 1935

The present system of taxation makes the farmer carry an unjust proportion of the cost of government. Our present tax system places 80 per cent of the tax burden on land and other general property. The Omnibus tax replacement program is a big step forward in the correction of this injustice.

Here is how taxes will be reduced:

1) Cut farm personal property and real estate taxes by 31% and cover the loss of revenue with replacement taxes such as sales tax, income tax, etc.
2) Country schools will receive 38% of the new school state aid revenues, shifted from the property tax.

3) Rural farming communities, who have suffered the most, will get most of the tax relief.
4) Pass a companion bill to limit the amount of general property taxes that can be levied.
5) New steps in tax equalization to spread the tax base and so increase the number sharing in the cost of government. By coupling increases in the net income tax rates and providing for a retail sales tax (as many other states have), the cost will be distributed in accordance with the ability to pay (foodstuffs to be exempted from sales tax).

          Constant Larson, President
          Alexandria, Minn.

FOR MINNESOTA SCHOOLS:
Taxation And School Support
Bulletin No. 3 February 1935
Published by: Minnesota Education Association

This Association continues to support it's FIVE-POINT PROGRAM developed last fall in response to our education crisis:
1) Enlarged school districts
2) State aid revision
3) Revision of tax delinquency laws
4) Improved and more equitable methods of assessment
5) Revenues to supplement, or in lieu of, property taxes

It should be pointed out that basic reform of any kind cannot be achieved overnight. Certainly, broad based support is essential. The schools after all belong to the people, not to those who work in them. It must be remembered that if new revenues are created, such changes must be supported by the citizens of the State, and their elected representatives.

We also feel compelled to point out that it is not possible to cure all the ills of the Depression through the invention of some formula. The general problem of taxation is too complex to make this possible. Proposals for a modern single tax or the advocacy merely of a high-rate general sales tax do not properly take into account the complexities of the general tax problem. The Committee recognizes that any general economic recovery would do more for the schools than could any special remedial legislation.

For the Executive Board by the Special Committee

          Floyd B. Moe, Chairman

San Rafael
Feb 14-35

Marcus,

Japanese and Communists are thick as flys in summer out here. Minnesota is also a hotbed of Communists so if you have a chance to strike a blow at them do so. I heard the American Legion talk on Lincoln birthday and they plan to go before all state lawmaking bodies and sound alarm.

If Governor Floyd B. Olson is not a Communist, he is not far off. So many folks think freedom is safe regardless of what happens.

I wish you were in Congress just now. So many things vital to our country are up for consideration. Perhaps you can go for it next time. Abraham Lincoln never attended law school, he learned the law by carefully reading law books. You have the mind so I see no reason why you cannot learn as much law as the rest. Not all well educated folks went to college.

Here is hoping for you. Our country needs all her loyal sons.

          Lots of love, Mamie

Mark Nolan
Rep. 61st District, Gilbert
WCCO Broadcast, Minneapolis
Friday, April 12th, 1935

The 1935 Legislative session will soon end and it's deeds or misdeeds will pass into history. Let us consider what has happened.

In January, the Conservatives secured control of the Legislature. Although this faction attempted to dress themselves in the new name of "Independent Progressives," the public soon discovered they represented the same reactionary element which, with the exception of 1933, had controlled the destinies of the State Legislature for fifty years.

Let us consider a few of the accomplishments of this Legislature. They proceeded on the Conservative agenda and now point with pride to their tax program, which was divided into two parts. Part one is the Constitutional Limitation Bill which is intended to eliminate property tax levies for state purposes; known as House File 444, it passed the House a few weeks ago. Part two is the Omnibus Tax Bill (H.F. 1564) which passed the House yesterday by a vote of 69 to 53.

Regards part one, the proponents of the Youngquist Tax Limitation Bill sobbed long and loudly about the heavy taxes paid by the small businessman, the farmer, and the poor home-owner, but it has been proved conclusively all over the United States that the greatest demand for such a law came not from the small home-owner, but from well organized real estate groups, many of whom care little or nothing about the needs of our government or schools, if they can escape in any manner the burden of taxation.

This leads us to part two, the notorious Tax Omnibus Bill which, although recently prepared, was given complete right of way over any tax proposals by Liberal Members. This bill proposes some increase in tax rates on Income, Mine Occupation, cigarettes, amusements, and Gross Earnings of telephone companies; the main revenue feature being a 3% retail sales tax.

Thus in a short time this evening I have attempted to point out the high spots in the record of the present session. It illustrates how a political faction aided by an editorial policy of an over-zealous press frightened the people of the state by cries of cooperative commonwealth, state socialism, and communism, and thus seized control of the law-making power of the state. They have used the Legislature, created to aid the public welfare, for the benefit of the few. And all this in the name of Americanism and Liberty.

EXECUTIVE AND OFFICIAL COMMUNICATION STATE OF MINNESOTA
Executive Department
St. Paul, April 24, 1935

Hon. G.W. Johnson
Speaker of the House
Dear Sir:

I am returning to you without my approval H.F. No. 1564 ("Omnibus Tax Bill"). I veto this bill on the principal ground that it is not based upon the means and ability of the persons taxed, to pay the taxes imposed. Those who can least afford to pay are taxed the most, and those who can most afford to pay are taxed the least, or not taxed at all.

Respectfully yours,
Floyd B. Olson,
Governor.

This was put out by a St. Paul organization called the "Minnesota Committee in Support of American Democracy".

Looking at the Legislature Broadcast
From: Minnesota News and Comment
A Weekly Column by
R.W. Hitchcock, St. Paul
Thursday evening, April 25th, 1935

Good evening, men and women of Minnesota - - Six months ago a new legislature was chosen. The people registered an emphatic "no" to the proposition of a co-operative commonwealth and to the reckless proposals of the Farmer-Labor platform to overthrow the present economic system, to stifle all free initiative, and to plunge the state into an orgy of governmental ownership, which in the end would cost the people not only their substance, but their liberties as well.

During the legislative session that ended this afternoon, millions were voted for relief. The beginnings of an adequate old age pension plan were made. Crime was grappled with by a comprehensive program of law enforcement. Increased funds for the public schools were voted and a beginning of what will soon radically change and enlarge public school support was made; but for the Governor's veto of the Omnibus Tax Bill that step would have been a tremendous stride forward. Ample funds for a vast state highway expansion are assured. The vital project of restoring stable lake levels made substantial headway. The mortgage moratorium law was reenacted. Compensation insurance was increased.

Yet despite these advances, the result of the Governor's veto is the tax rate on property leaps upward, and mountains of new tax burdens are mercilessly piled on the back of the home and property owner.

Tax reform was the session's supreme issue but these intolerable conditions, the Governor says to the people of Minnesota, must continue. Nay more, he says to his people, you haven't seen anything yet; I will make you to suffer as you have never before until you think your back is broken. I will harden my heart, says the Governor's veto, and I will do this unto you and more also.

The Legislature labored long and earnestly but all their efforts fall short, far short, of producing the revenue the state must have. It is the program described in the Omnibus Tax Bill to which the state must come back to. The Governor's veto simply postpones the day of relief.

MINNEAPOLIS JOURNAL
Saturday, April 27, 1935
Editorial -

"OUR STUDIOUS LEGISLATORS"

One of the last official acts of the Minnesota legislature was the creation of a commission to study the state's tax system and to seek new sources of revenue to replace existing levies. In light of what was accomplished in behalf of tax relief at the last session, this gesture is nothing if not ironic.

When the legislature adjourned, it left the taxpayer worse off than he was when that body convened in January. Not only was almost nothing done to relieve the burden on real estate, the legislature set a new high record for expenditures. The property levy of 14.95 mills is likewise the highest mill rate ever authorized. With that as it's major contribution to taxpayer relief, it is entirely fitting that another "study" of the tax structure be authorized. The fact that the state has always at it's service a staff of tax experts in the state tax commission, whose recommendations the legislature consistently ignores, ensures the taxpayer that while his plight may go unrelieved, it will not lack for scholarly examination.

Palladio Bldg, Duluth
May 15th, 1935

Marcus,

I want to thank you for the pleasant time I spent with you last week at "Restful Inn." Coming home on the bus I jotted down some thoughts that had come to me as I roamed "around Sandy at the mouth of the Prairie." At home I put them in better shape and type them hereon:

Where Lake meets the "Old Fur Traders Trail,
    that reaches Sandy Lake by way of the
    Savanne
There I stopped and reminisced,
    of the Courage of Man

For here passed in the days of long ago,
    canoes of bold Voyageurs seeking
    another world
Where lakes, hills, and timber,
    and rolling prairies unfurled

From Montreal and Gitchee Gumee, Priests on
    peaceful Christian Missions came this way
Here Chippewa Indians held
    fighting Sioux at bay.
On Battle Island evidence of fighting still
    remains, where Red Sioux and Chippewa
    bled
Where one may yet find stone axe,
    and flint arrow head
Across Sandy Lake from where I stood,
    savage Indians warred in brutal might
Here Priests, Trappers, Indians in peace,
    camped for the night.

My reveries come to sudden end,
    discordant rattles of loose bridge plank
      rend the quiet span;
        An auto honks where Lake
          met that "Trail of Early Man."

Sincerely,
Jim Finch

LARSON BOAT WORKS

OUTBOARD MOTORS
SALES AND SERVICE

PAUL G. LARSON
ROY B. LARSON

BUILDERS OF OUTBOARD MOTOR BOATS
ROWBOATS   -   DUCK BOATS
Boats Built to Order   -   Boat Supplies

Little Falls, Minnesota

May 9, 1935

Mr. Marcus Nelson,
McGregor, Minnesota

Dear Sir:

The 16 ft. boat you ordered is about ready. It is in the paint
room now and will be in nice shape to handle by the 13th. The 14 ft.
boats are in the making and we can possibly have one for you by the 13th
or 14th.

We are way short of the Fisherman's Choice model and Standard
Models. We are working one crew days and one nights on these boats and still
cannot supply the demand. It just seems that every one buying boats this
year have waited until recently to order. We have sold more boats already
than for several years this early in the season.

Yours very truly,

LARSON BOAT WORKS

By *Paul G. Larson,*

PL:CKL

"A Larson Boat Is Always Afloat"

*With greatly improved roads, Marcus, like all northern Minnesota resorters,
was enjoying a strong increase in the tourism business.*

San Rafael
May 17-35

Myrtle & Marcus,

Orvis took me up yesterday in a sleek B-10 Bomber. Was wonderful my first time up in an airplane. Had a time to get on my parachute I don't see how the boys deal with them and still fly. Lt. Claire Peterson, is from Fargo, flew as other pilot. Went up & down San Francisco Bay and flew over Alcatraz federal prison at height of 50 feet. That was something. I did not want to come down. ha.

United Air Lines is to take Orvis on as temporary First Officer about 30th of June. He expects they would start him on the Chicago to Newark run. Army seems not to care if boys stay or go so better he gets away from them.

When Orvis leaves here I will come home.
Mom

Above, Mamie and Orvis prepare to board the B-10.

At right, with Lt. Peterson. Notice the "Jiggs" squadron insignia above Mamie's head.

ALCATRAZ ISLAND - SAN FRANCISCO BAY

Nelson's Camp
May 22, 1935

Son & Wife,

Fishing good - have to beat the walleyes off with an oar. Been loafing like a professional.

Orvis, you asked of my work in the legislature. I authored or co-authored 27 bills, 7 of them passed the House but did not become law. I co-authored 7 other bills, and was sole author of another, that passed the House & Senate and were signed into law by the Governor. Here they are -

- H.F. 50 [General Law R8]. We legalized the counties right to make sales of tax anticipation certificates of indebtedness.
- H.F. 83 [General Law R4]. We passed a resolution memorializing the U.S. Congress to enact legislation to protect American Industry & Employees against cheap foreign labor and products.
- H.F. 162 [General Law C108]. We defined Manslaughter in the first degree & safeguarded the rights of the unborn.
- H.F. 264 [General Law C216]. Got better regulation & supervision at our packing plants & slaughter houses. Gave authority to Railroad & Warehouse Commissioner to inspect, etc.
- H.F. 311 [General Law C244]. Was sole author. Legalized certain sales of state land to earn revenue.
- H.F. 444 [General Law C394]. This bill proposes to amend the Minnesota Constitution so as to eliminate the tax on real and tangible personal property for state purposes. This is the most important work I've done so far. The voters will finally decide the issue.
- H.F. 768 [General Law C386]. Related to the sale and easing of certain delinquent tax lands acquired by the state.
- H.F. 1139 [General Law R17]. A resolution memorializing Congress to appropriate $125,000 for relief of schools in Minnesota.

Of course the Veto on the tax bill has really put us in a bind and there is no question but what we will have to go to a special session, probably in December.

Dad

STATE OF MINNESOTA
Department of Conservation
Saint Paul
June 7, 1935

C/O Big Sandy Lake
Honorable Marcus Nelson:

As I wrote to Messrs. Hodgin, Wotring, Miller, Moush, and Sather of your community, Section 5563 of the Minnesota Statutes specifically provides that no net or seine used for the taking of minnows shall be more than twenty-five feet in length or more than three feet in depth. It seems to me that if minnows have become so scarce that they cannot be procured by means of a legal size net then it is time that we cease to secure minnows or we cannot expect to maintain an adequate food supply for the game fish. I imagine without game fish in the waters of Big Sandy Lake that your resort business would soon end.

I very much regret that we do not look at the conservation of our wild life in the same way in which you and the resort keepers of Big Sandy Lake view it.

T. Surber
Superintendent, Fish Propagation

HYDE PARK HOTEL
Chicago
August 31-35

Darling Myrtle,

Dad & I arrived here at 8 A.M. yesterday and Orvis was waiting at the Union train station for us. He just in from landing at Chicago Municipal Airport. This is Hotel he lives in as do many other United people. He been overworked this week - First Officer must fly 100 hours a month but Captain only 80.

We arrived in Mpls at 9:30 in evening and made the crack flyer at 11:30. Dad had tickets and while I was reading went into men's room and got to gabbing with a man who makes a mouse trap and did not come too till almost train pulling out. Believe me I was getting nervous as I did not know where he went. Next time I'll carry my own ticket.

O. has to go back out to Newark on Tues. and we are going to see Carr in Springfield, Ohio as he is feeling poorly. Dad is anxious to see him.

The bomber I went up in was demolished in a crash by some new regular officer - $70,000.00 gone bluey.

Well, Dad opened all his mail from past week on train and lo and behold was official word he is to get another settlement from 1918 fire. After all these years they finally are to give closer to what everyone lost. Ought to amount to 8 or 10 thousand dollars. Can sure use it, as Dad owes practically everybody.

Orvis just came in to our room with a basket of nice apples to take to Carr. They are swell. Won't the old man be surprised?

Mom

P.S. This morning had a fancy haircut by some guy. Cost 60 cts.

"Minnesota News And Comment"
By R.W. Hitchcock
November 21, 1935

The special session of the Legislature called for December 2nd is limited as to it's length and as to matters to be considered only by the will of the session itself. It can only be hoped the discussion will be confined to 1) social security legislation to dovetail with the federal Social Security Act and 2) the unsettled tax problem. The fact that members must pay their own expenses, however, is a powerful deterrent.

AITKIN INDEPENDENT AGE
November 22, 1935

SANDY LAKE -
The Bell Horn Bay PTA met at the school with a fine crowd in attendance. The school was recently connected with the electric highline from McGregor and one of the features of the evening was the presentation of an electric clock to Miss Myrtle Nelson's room.

Aitkin Public Schools
November 29, 1935

Mr. Nelson:
The Board of Education is very, very much against the idea of taking the income tax and using it for any other purpose than the schools. We feel that the schools are of enough importance to warrant very drastic action on the part of the Legislature when it comes to the changing of the income tax in any tax reform package you may pass.

L.C. Murray, Superintendent

Maurice J. Salisbury
Rabey, Minn.
12-4-35

Marcus,

I suppose you are pretty busy down there in Saint Paul. I notice they are swinging over to your plan of allowing the delinquent taxes to be settled in installments over ten years. Do you think it will go all the way through?

Was looking through the paper again and see you are on the sub-committee for the old age pension. Well, do the best you can Marcus. You'll be old yourself some day.

M.J.S.

County Home, Aitkin
Dec 9 - 35

Hon. Marcus Nelson:

This is just a few words in remembrance of your obligation what you promised us when you were here trying to get votes you said you were in favor of and old age pension.

Now you have a chance to do it this week.

yours very truly

Jacob Swanson

Hyde Park Hotel
Dec 18, 1935

Folks,

We are using the new Douglas DC-2's more and more all the time. Has greater range, etc. than the Boeing 247, so of course that changes schedules, routes, and so on.

Looks like I won't get laid off after all. Week after week the junior co-pilots were getting let go, until I was the last one left. Then, just a few days ago, business picked up & I hear now they are even calling a couple of the boys back. A relief all around.

Hope Dad is getting some good things done in St. Paul.

Orv

HOUSE OF REPRESENTATIVES
Saint Paul
January 22, 1936

Mr. L.C. Murray
Aitkin Superintendent of Schools
Sir:

I will do everything I can to assist in getting an appropriation from the state to maintain a high

---

State of Minnesota
HOUSE of REPRESENTATIVES
GEORGE W. JOHNSON, SPEAKER
SAINT PAUL

MARCUS NELSON
54TH DISTRICT
TAMARACK, MINN.

December 12, 1935

Mr. Jacob Swanson
C/O Aitkin County Home
Sir:

I have the letter signed by you and all of the boys and am very glad to hear from you as we are working on the thing that you are so vitally interested in.

It has been hard to get the other members to understand just what is necessary in order to get out a workable bill. The most we can expect under the present setup is $30.00 a month and this will be based upon the need of the applicant.

You can rest assured that I am keeping you in mind and that I am doing everything in my power to make the pension workable.

Please extend my greetings to all the boys there.

Marcus Nelson

UNITED AIR LINES "3-MILE-A-MINUTE" MULTI-MOTORED BOEING

*The 10-passenger Boeing 247, the first "modern" airliner.
Below shows the United Air Lines system in 1935.*

school dormitory in Aitkin if I happen to be returned here in 1937, when the next regular session meets. You must understand it is quite out of the question to bring up the matter during this Special Session. With the old age pension bill a law, I feel we can discontinue the county home and I cannot think of any better use of the building than to put it into a dormitory and take care of those children who are running wild around Aitkin during the school year.

    Marcus Nelson

Winter Park, Florida
Jan. 30, 1936

Marcus:-

    I am very much pleased your bill covering the installment plan of paying taxes on delinquent land passed the House & Senate. Am quite sure you did a great deal of work for the bill and hope it will do a lot of good. I am not ashamed to say it will help me a great deal.

    I am thinking of all those years on this very day I was freezing my a-- off in a dark camp in the deep woods and now as I write this I am basking in the tropical sun holding a cool drink.

    C.P. DeLaittre

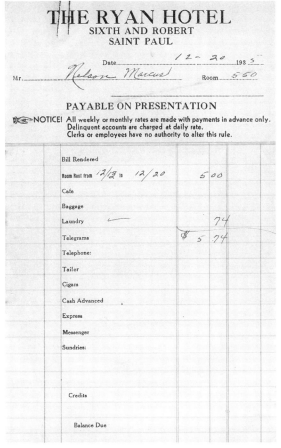

*Marcus always stayed at this hotel when
the legislature was in session.*

Bell Horn Bay School
Sat, Feb 22nd, 1936

Orv,

Finished cleaning up what the janitor missed and decided to grade papers, etc. here instead of dragging the stuff home.

A couple of my adopted "Chippewa Kids" dropped by. They are my favorites; little Annie Goodsky & her baby brother Pee-chee-wah-nee. It was so cute to watch Annie towing Pee around in their little wagon. I have been teaching them Ojibway on the sly. Queer that a white person is teaching Indian's their own language but Goodsky's want their children to make good in the white world & of course until recently the government has long pushed the idea that they give up their Indian ways. But it seems a shame for them to let it all go. I only

HAROLD KNUTSON

COMMITTEE:
WAYS AND MEANS

HOME ADDRESSES:
ST. CLOUD, MINN.
WADENA, MINN.

CONGRESS OF THE UNITED STATES

HOUSE OF REPRESENTATIVES

WASHINGTON, D.C.

January 7, 1936

Hon. Marcus Nelson,
House of Representatives,
St. Paul, Minnesota.

Dear Marcus:

Thank you for your good letter of January 3d and I want you to know that I deeply appreciate your interest.

After I saw you at the Capitol someone told me that Hjalmer Peterson would file for congress in the event that he does not file for governor. In view of this I think it will be all right to have our friend from Aitkin file. He will not be satisfied until he has had his fling and there is nothing like getting over with it early. You know what I mean.

I am coming home for the state and district conventions, and I would like very much to see you at that time and talk matters over in greater detail.

Kindest regards and best wishes,

Sincerely,
Harold Knutson

Pee and Annie at the old Indian Village on the north side of Big Sandy Lake.

Myrtle described her new outfit thus: "black wool crepe hat, black dress with bright red satin belt, sleeve trim, little side trims at top."

Myrtle's room at the Bell Horn Bay School in January, 1936.

Bulletin and Reading Corner. Peter Peterson (L) and
Kenneth Engh - leaders on honor roll.

recently learned the Chippewa came from the East originally and were "cousins" to the Powhatans. Both are from the Algonquian group.

The R.E.A. is coming to Aitkin County and, boy, are people out in the country excited. The towns have long had the electric, yet the poor old farmers still sit in the dark when the sun goes down. We got a highline to the school last November, but most of Shamrock Town is still waiting. Dad has some meetings scheduled in March to get the community organized and get things moving.

Do you remember that funny old biddy Mrs. Johnson? She showed up at a PTA meeting (why I don't know, her kids are long gone) and when somebody asked her to turn on the light she got red in the face & walked away. Turns out she wouldn't touch the switch because she was afraid she'd be electrocuted!

Myrtle

P.S. I am enclosing snap of my nice new black outfit. I needed a good dress desperately.

*Mamie brings Orvis up-to-date on Sandy Lake happenings. As she so often did,
she asked him to return this postcard for her collection. Jan. 25, 1936.*

Hyde Park Hotel,
Room 805
April 7-36

Darling Myrtle,

Arrived here this morning well rested. I paid 25 cents for a pillow and slept as much in the chair as I would have in a pullman bed. I got Orvis on the phone and took a cab to the electric station. 15 cents to come within two blocks. Orvis was on call so had to go to field.

I ate a nice sandwich downstairs. Ham with some kind dressing on it. Was good but cost enough to be good.

Almost as cold as Duluth here. This room is none too warm. Seems to face north and can see open lake to the east.

I hope I can get into the Art Institute school right away. Do my visiting in Indiana when weather gets better.

I hope your Dad was not unreasonable about the money I had to have. He always wants to cabbage every penny I'm ever close to. I feel he should let me know all he had expected before he was wanting it.

Mom

P.S. He seems to think income from Indiana farm is his before it is mine.

Mpls
April 16, 1936

Mr. Orvis and Miss Myrtle Nelson:

Enclosed find a Satisfaction of Mortgage on the 8 acre parcel of land & buildings at the mouth of the Prairie River on Big Sandy Lake. Upon presentation of this document and your quit claim deed to the Register of Deeds in Aitkin, a Warranty Deed to same will be issued in your names.

Dolph Bezoier

State of Minnesota
HOUSE OF REPRESENTATIVES
April 22, 1936

Friend Marcus,

The top of the morning to you. I have not heard any thing about how you fare since we left the Capitol but I trust that all is well.

I am lately directing my energies to the business of trying to capture enough of this world's wealth to keep going without jeopardizing my interests in the world to come. Just now I have a strong German farmer with an industrious wife and three young children who is expecting to get a soldier's bonus of $300.00 and wants to buy a farm in your part of the state. This man is inured to hardship & work and will attend strictly to his business. I told him I would send him to you for more information as you know land and corners better than any man in that country. He is a decent fellow and will heed what you tell him.

George W. Champlin
8th District, Lake Crystal

P.S. Are you intending to run for the House again? I hope so. I am going to file and if I am successful I shall not feel right unless you are among those present.

Marshall-Wells Co.
Duluth
May 26, 1936

Mr. Nelson:

As you of course must know Marshall-Wells now owns your old store building at Tamarack, occupied by Byron Osterman for the past several months. While glad to have Mr. Osterman in the building as a tenant, what we really want to do is sell the property. We thought Mr. Heller might be interested but he has put up a Red & White grocery on the lot next door. Have you any idea where a possible purchaser might be reached? Do you think you might interest anyone in the property? We would, of course, expect to make reasonable payment to anyone consummating a sale.

C.E. Madison

*These fishermen were so successful, this photo
was used in promotions for years.
One hopes there were more in party – there
are nearly sixty walleyes on the long stringer!*

On the Prairie with a nice stringer of mostly walleyes.

*Those without boats could fish off the shore with very long
and inexpensive bamboo poles.*

*Deerhunter near the mouth of the
Prairie River.*

at Nelson's Camp

AIR VIEW OF BELL HORN BAY, BIG SANDY LAKE, MINNESOTA

A postcard used by the Camp after World War Two.

Two beautiful northern pike speared through the ice on Big Sandy Lake. Mamie had a promotional postcard made from it.

Maurice Nelson having lunch on Battle Island while hunting ducks on Big Sandy Lake.

The little house keeps the spear fisherman warm and excludes light from his large spearing hole, enabling a clear view in the usually six to eight feet of water.

MR. FARMER, MR. TAXPAYER

Mr. Citizen of Aitkin County:—

Do you want legislation that will stamp you a criminal if you improve your own property? Do you favor a law where a farmer with no barn could not build a barn; a farmer with no cattle could not put cattle on his farm; a farmer's crop acreage could not be increased over 100 per cent even though his last crop was only a garden patch; a farmer or settler leaving his place for a period of more than two years could not return to his own land to live?

These drastic, dangerous and confiscatory provisions were embodied in a bill known as S. F. No. 1035 and introduced by the Farmer-Labor minority during the 1935 session of the legislature. The bill was introduced by request of the State Administration Department of Conservation. If passed it would have applied to approximately one half of Aitkin county as well as other large areas in Northern Minnesota.

Drastic as S. F. No. 1035 may seem, it is merely consistent and in accord with the present administration's policy of state ownership and the building of a vast public domain of our Northern Minnesota's land and recreational resources. For several years an insidious and persistent attempt has been made and is being made to force land into tax delinquency by high taxes, and subsequently to have tax delinquent lands revert to the state in absolute ownership, to be developed and administered by a large army of public employes at the taxpayers' expense.

Your attention is called to the map of Aitkin county on the other side. Note that more than fifty per cent of the gross area of Aitkin county has been set aside as prospective public domain. Approximately ten per cent of the lands within these areas are reverted state trust lands, which, in accordance with the present state land use policy, have been withdrawn from sale and consequently from future agricultural development. It is further proposed that as lands revert to the state for nonpayment of taxes, they be withdrawn from sale, placed on the tax exempt list and dedicated to the creation of a permanent wilderness.

Lake shore property owned by the state and exempt from all taxes is being developed and improved at the taxpayers' expense and leased (not sold) to the public for recreational and summer home purposes in direct competition with property owned and developed by private endeavor and initiative.

Think these matters over and then decide if you want Farmer-Labor government with ultimate public ownership.

MINNESOTA **N**EEDS **N**ELSON

Issued and circulated by the Aitkin County Republican Committee, C. S. Lind, Chairman, Aitkin, Minn.

Tingdale Bros.
June 12, 1936

Mr. Marcus Nelson, Big Sandy Lake, Minn.
(Mouth of Prairie River via McGregor, reached by Highway #65 -- turn to the right at Sather's Store before reaching Sandy Lake and follow the road to Marcus Nelson's restaurant.)

Dear Marcus:

This will introduce Mr. Philip Elofson.
Please show him some cheap land. He is in the market for 40 acres. Any favor you can show Mr. Elofson will be greatly appreciated.

Yours truly,

TINGDALE BROS., INC.

BY: Martin Tingdale, Pres.

Copy to: Mr. Philip Elofson

Aitkin
June 16, 1936

Marcus,

House District #54 Primary Election results as follows:

G.W. Alfs	904
Isedor Iverson	1,388
Marcus Nelson	1,376

We had better prepare for a hard fight this fall against Iverson & the Farm-Laborites. They are coming back strong from their set-back in '34.

C.S. Lind

H.B. Fryberger
Duluth
June 18, 1936

Mr. Nelson:-

I was out to Sandy Lake today and drove over the road where the so-called graveling was done. You were to have one-half dozen loads of gravel put in that roadway, as I recall it. I estimated there was about one load of gravel scattered about, which didn't amount to anything - - in fact, I am afraid the partridges, if there were more than two coveys raised in the nearby woods this summer, will eat the gravel all up. Just what did your man claim he did, any way?

H.B.F.

AITKIN REPUBLICAN
August 27, 1936

- OLSON FUNERAL -

Representative Marcus Nelson attended the funeral obsequies for Governor Olson held at the Minneapolis Municipal Auditorium and the internment at Lakewood Cemetery. The new Governor, Hjalmar Petersen, proclaimed a 30 day mourning period. On Monday last, 15,000 persons paid their respects as the body lay in state in the Capitol Rotunda.

Pelican Rapids, Minn.
August 28, 1936

Hon. Marcus Nelson:

Friday, September 11th, is Legislative Day at the Minnesota State Fair. For a number of years it has been customary for as many of the House members as possible to get together for a dinner meeting. It is suggested that we meet at the Ryan Hotel at 6:30 Thursday evening, September 10th.

In this way we would have a chance to renew acquaintances and talk over the situation in our different districts as well as discuss some of the issues which predominate in the campaign.

Trusting your campaign is coming along to your satisfaction and that we will have the pleasure of your good company on the evening of the 10th.

    Roy E. Dunn
    Rep., 50th District

P.S. I enclose remarks we have prepared regarding the Farmer-Labor platform. Feel free to use any of it in your canvassing.

For use by Legislative candidates:
FARMER-LABOR PLATFORM

It is worthwhile to compare their 1936 program with the program and plan used in 1934.

You will recall that the 1934 Farmer-Labor platform was a very radical document. It called for a cooperative commonwealth -- the socialization of all systems of transportation and communication, key industries, banks, packing plants, natural resources and utilities. It declared that capitalism had failed and proposed a complete revolution of the American Economic system.

So confident were the leaders of the party that the people would accept this proposition, they not only forced their state candidates to stand on the platform, but they made a bold bid for control of the Legislature, endorsing candidates freely. They refused to endorse any candidate who so much as hesitated in his acceptance of the full dose.

It isn't news that the result of the 1934 election was a big disappointment to the radicals of the state. Their legislative candidates fell by the score, and they came up to the legislative session with only a corporal's guard to speak for them. By reason of a split vote they were able to win several state offices, but in all majority elections, where the issue of radicalism was clear-cut, they failed.

At the outset of the 1936 campaign, the public was given to understand that the Farmer-Labor party wasn't going to be quite so bold. It's platform was couched in milder language, and legislative endorsements were fewer and farther between.

But the official news organ of the F-L party assures it's subscribers that what appears to be a change in policy isn't really that at all. In other words, it is admitted that the party is just as radical as ever. Further, the national communist party has publicly endorsed the Farmer-Labor candidates of Minnesota. So the people need be under no illusions as to the convictions and intentions of the F-L party. It's leaders frankly boast of them, and who are we not to believe them!

McGregor, Minn.
Aug 31 - 1936

Markus Nelson
State Representative
Sir:

would you sometimes when you call into Tamarack around the 10th of Sept. at Paul Hellers store I will leave a application blank there for Old Age Pension. to testify that you know me since year of 1897 as a settler of Aitkin Co.

I will have the Papers there on or before that Date and Oblige,

    yours very truly
    Oscar Sundberg

P.S. how is Political field

Indypls
Monday, Sept 28, 1936

Myrtle,

I haven't seen your Mom since last Monday. She has been gallivanting around the country side for weeks. Have quite a stack of mail for her, another thick one from your Dad I see. I was sure I had mentioned to her there were letters from Marcus but maybe not.

Your Mom has been seeing to getting the family lands worked out better, so less complicated. Some hurt feelings in some quarters but I suppose unavoidable with so many of us. She wants to wind up with Grandpa Ambrose Barnett's original farm as her's alone. Be clear of everyone else. O.K. by me and I think that's way it will finally go.

I heard Landon give a speech. He is a good speaker but not so good as F.D.R. according to my lights.

    Aunt Dilla

Breeze Hill
Sandy Lake
Sat Nite, Oct 3, 1936

Mom,

Have had quite a few mice in the cabin. Roy will trap them for me this coming week. Dad wants me to eat down at his cafe so I won't be putting out for food.

Thompson is putting a chimney in the restaurant and they will move in there Monday to look after the place for Dad. Dad will cook in his own cabin by the river. The other day, he carved a name for it on a board & hung it on the door - the "Wanigan," after the river drive houseboats. He's been down in the dumps and says he has not heard from you since you left, which I guess is understandable with the way things are. He went out campaigning tonight. I guess there is something he has to go to almost every day or night until the election.

School is the same. I'm really in a rut at Bell Horn. I've definitely decided to go somewhere else next school year.

Myrtle

Mamie in her little Nashville house.

Aitkin
Nov 5, 1936

Marcus,

General Election results as follows:

Isedor Iverson	3,168 votes
Marcus Nelson	2,880 votes

Iverson was swept in on Roosevelt's coat-tails. Farmer-Labor candidates made a strong showing throughout the county and state and will likely be organizing the House next January.

We were just on the wrong side of the fence this time.

Carl Lind

Nashville, Indiana
Nov 8-36

Marcus -

I received your letters but haven't felt ready to answer but Myrtle wrote again so guess I better.

I had always intended to build a permanent home there at the lake but I got out of the notion when I heard about the carrying on of you and some of your friends from Hill City, Mpls. and so on. I was foolish enough to think that was all past, but I guess you have been kind of roped in, I should judge from what I hear.

I made an investigation and found out more than I had cared to believe and since this Mrs. Williams woman had the nerve to come to the Camp when Myrtle was there, I figured I'd better fade out of the picture. I do not think you can blame me for that.

I am building a little house on a corner of my land I bought near Nashville. I have been painting some and find I can have a life of my own here among this little colony of artists. I hope that you keep well and that Myrtle does too. It was very hard to leave her up there but is no place there for me. She wrote she did not know but was afraid the election was not going so good. Sure hope it does. They do not realize what you did for them in way of old age pension. Here, very few get it.

As ever, Mamie

Tingdale Bros.
November 17, 1936

Mr. J.V. Anderson, Mpls:

Regards your inquiry, there is a good sawmill and complete outfit in a location you desire. This is owned by Marcus Nelson, Tamarack, Minn. As this party intends to go to Newark, New Jersey for several weeks to visit his son, feel assured that if you make a quick connection with him, you may be able to get his complete outfit for $650.00.

Martin Tingdale

Copy to: Mr. Marcus Nelson

Marcus, I see your Constitutional Amendment #2 was soundly defeated by the voters. What do we do now about getting rid of that damn state levy on property taxes?

John B. Hamilton
General Contractor, Indypls
Dec 11 1936

Cousin Myrtle,

How is the "Schoolmarm" these days anyhow?

Saw Orv awhile last Sat. afternoon. Mother and I were getting ready to go to the store when a plane made a turn over the house rather low, so we went outside and saw it was headed for Fort Harrison. Was not sure it was Orv as he usually spends more time over house, so we waited until he had time to land and I called the field. They said he was there and put him on phone. He had so short time to stay

Marcus and First Officer (co-pilot) Nelson.

Mom & I went out to the field and as he was hungry we visited in a hamburger joint. Said had no passengers & was bringing the ship back to Chicago. He put on a little show for us and was gone.

Sunday P.M. Aunt Mamie paid us one of those flying visits which seems to be a "Nelson Characteristic," just can't stay awhile but have to keep moving on & on, but even if they are always in a hurry we are glad to have them come as often as they will.

Aunt Mamie said you were coming down for Holidays, so we will be expecting you. She also plans to entertain you in her new home in Brown County.

I will send this to Santa Claus, Ind. so they can cancel the stamp and send it to you.

John B.H.

Mamie & Myrtle (center) boarding a flight on United's DC-3, the "State of New York". They were able to travel on a pass, space-available.

88

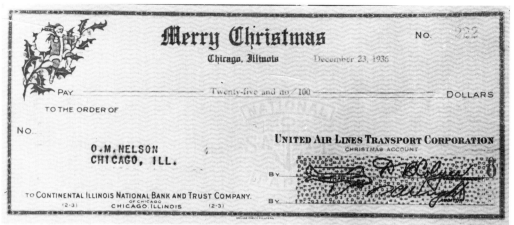

Merry Christmas

Chicago, Illinois December 23, 1936

NO. 922

PAY — Twenty-five and no/100 — DOLLARS

TO THE ORDER OF

NO.

O.M. NELSON
CHICAGO, ILL.

UNITED AIR LINES TRANSPORT CORPORATION
CHRISTMAS ACCOUNT

BY

BY

TO CONTINENTAL ILLINOIS NATIONAL BANK AND TRUST COMPANY.
OF CHICAGO
CHICAGO, ILLINOIS   (2-3)
(2-3)

Newark N.J. Athletic Club
Sunday Dec 20th, 1936

Dad,

Still working this "Hell Stretch." Made two round trips from Chicago in two days. After Xmas, I should have better trips as I am flying with two of the most senior pilots. Word is we are to get the new DC-3 on our run. It's even bigger and better than the DC-2. We can carry 21 passengers and fly the route non-stop.

I enjoyed our visit & glad I was able to get a pass for your return to Chicago. You did right to just sit there and wait for that seat - I had a hunch one would open up. You must write & tell me how you liked your first plane ride. My only regret is that I couldn't have been your pilot and enjoy it with you!

Orvis

P.S. Heard from Mom. She sounds well. Myrtle is there & was covering her chairs.

Nelson's Camp
Sunday Jan 17, 1937

Mom -

Dad has been sick in bed with a cold for a week. He was staying at the Willard in Aitkin until Thurs. & couldn't get along any longer by himself so he came home and I have been doctoring him. He was better today.

Sorry you think Indiana isn't good for you either. Mightn't it be better if your house had a furnace? We should try to be together next winter. Too lonesome for both of us this way.

Myrtle

P.S. Heard a good one Friday -

Supt. of Schools to Teacher: "Did you take your salary to the bank?"

Teacher: "Yes, it was too small to go by itself."

Nashville, Ind.
Jan 25-37

Myrtle,

This flood is terrible. They are appealing for help all the time. Some damage was done to my road and it's too damp to cross so I will have to wait. I am at a loss what to do. I think will have to rent a place down the road, woman there seems all right.

I am so disgusted with the way the water comes here. I do not think I will stay another winter. When weather gets better, will finish my house and try to sell. If Maggie's get rested (they wore themselves out butchering) I may go there and finish her pictures.

Darling, I wish I were with you.

Mom

Springfield, Ohio
April 17 1937

Friend Marcus,

I am still eating yet and am still on my weary way. The morning of life is spent and the sun is going down and I am like poor Fido laying in the shade swatting at the flys and dreaming of the battles I won. And I have won as many battles as the fat racketeers and the enemys of society ever won. Am trying to keep away from my enemys as I travel through the wilderness to the Land of Canaan. You know they don't count Mile Posts in Canaan, don't have Decoration Days, no bathing beauties for side show, or Sunflower Parade, just happiness and no grief added to it.

I don't think I would care much about going back to Minn. I got all the traveling I want & will stay put here. I would like to see the old fishing hole and take one more trip up the river with our dinner and shake your old paw and say good bye but I don't never expect to.

Dennis A. Carr

*The much beloved Dennis Carr
"in the late afternoon of life"*

Nelson's Camp
May 24, 1937

Mom,

Very happy you have decided to put your place in Nashville up for rent and are coming back home. Don't wear yourself out with the move, better to leave things behind for now if necessary.

Dad gave a fine welcome to PTA - told 'em first school in Minnesota was on Sandy Lake in 1832 at the American Fur Company Trading Post, so he supposed the first parent-teacher meeting was there too! He really enjoyed getting the hanky from you for his birthday. Showed it to me first thing. I gave him a night shirt. Things have changed significantly for the better around here.

Dad paid for plowing and is planting garden for me. I can pay my full share of expense this summer & we'll manage to live pretty cheaply.

All the fishing cabins were rented this weekend. Mosquitoes are getting worse right on schedule.

Myrtle

Nelson's Camp
July 2-37

My Darling Son,

Am at Myrtle's little cabin for through the weekend and then expect to move over to my log cabin on lake. Marcus to stay in Wanigan.

Dad seemed glad to see me. Today I made a chicken dinner and Myrtle made a peach cobbler and did Dad ever eat. I guess we all did. We listened to him tell of his comings and goings most of afternoon. He had some new stories you know the kind he likes to tell.

I went down to sketch the bridge with setting sun in background. Will make a pretty picture. They have re-built it and looks a solid span now - still all wood but hold more weight than old.

Mom

Hyde Park Hotel
July 21, 1937

Mom,

Well, what a day! Got in last nite and five of us senior co-pilots tried to decide whether to quit and go with North West Air Lines. They need experienced pilots badly and said would make us Captains in a short time. After a lot of hand wringing, I finally decided to stay with United.

$8,000 a year against $3,000 wasn't to be turned down lightly. But so many things enter into it that I believe that I will be better off 10 years from now with United than I would with North West. I hope I didn't guess wrong.

Boy, we certainly stunned the company. They talked to us for an hour this morning telling us their side of the story. Cahill got on the telephone with R.T. Freng, United's Chief of Flying, and opened up with both barrels. Cahill listened for a while with a funny expression on his face and then turned to me saying, "Here, you take it. He's jabbering Norwegian." So I took the phone and got some order restored.

They were frank that we would all soon be 1st pilots with United and that they had a big investment in us and hated to see us go. Besides they can hardly replace us for they have about everyone on Douglas airplanes that can be. Our future here with the big Douglas ships (N.W. uses mostly the smaller Lockheed Electras) convinced all but one of us to turn down the offer.

Orvis

Hyde Park Hotel
Sept 5th, 1937

Folks,

I think you said today is the day Mom & Myrtle move up to LaPorte. Hope all goes O.K. and that Myrtle likes her new school.

Myrtle, you and I are now the proud owners of a Stinson Monocoupe. The guy had to sell and between your available cash and mine there was a total of $800 and he took it. It's a fine high-winged ship - 4 passenger, single radial engine, with closed cabin. I took it up this morning and the engine really purrs. I'm planning to fly it up to Tamarack for my vacation later this month. Will see if Dilla & John & maybe Floyd Cyrus want to come along.

Mom, I took care of your car mortgage and am sending the papers back to you.

Orv

P.S. Looks like I'm going to be sent to the West Coast.

LaPorte, Minn.
Oct 8-37

Marcus -

Myrtle wants you to bring up her mattress when you come. It's on top of bed in her cabin and has a mattress cover on it. Also a black cloth coat in bedroom. We have a good small drop leaf table now so all we really need inside is the mattress.

Orvis is fine and in Seattle. He is to fly the Seattle - Vancouver - Portland - Oakland run. Found a lot of boys he used to know in Army and two of the head pilots are boys from Robert Fulton School in Mpls. Can you beat that. He was so tired & disappointed as he wanted on the trans-continental line but he may get his opening for head pilot there sooner.

I am fixing to enamel Myrtle's dresser as it's an awful looking thing now. I think you better bring the 3 covers off that bed too, Marcus. Then will have a bed for you here.

Mamie & Myrtle

P.S. I have to run down to my place in Nashville. Tenant no good.

Edinburg, Ind.
Oct 20, 1937

C/O Nashville, Ind.

Sister Mamie,

Well, Orvis came in his "Stinson" and picked up Dilla & Johnny and flew to Chicago to pick up Orvis' friend, Floyd Cyrus. Mr. Cyrus told her Orvis loaned him $1,200 and got him the mechanic job at United and so you can be sure he speaks awful highly of your son.

They landed after dark on Sat. in a field so. of Tamarack. Dilla could not see a thing and said Orvis must have cat eyes, scared her some I think. Mr. Cyrus went to see his folks & Marcus took his place in the plane and they all flew up to LaPorte to visit Myrtle. Dilla just raved over the beautiful blue lakes and fall colors - said the whole north part of state looked like was all water did not seem the same when viewed from the ground. They went home next day. I got a card from Myrtle saying she had been worried about Orvis flying back all nite w/o rest but Dilla said he is a pretty tough boy & they had no trouble. He slept a few hours at Dilla's and then took off for Seattle!

Cora Musselman

P.S. They turned the Electric Light on at Mag's last nite & we went over to see how it is. Looked like some City home, the lights all over the house & outside. The light at garage lights up to the barn. Zelma's was on too but I haven't seen it yet.

LaPorte
Sunday Nite, Nov 7, 1937

Orv,

Hope you heard Charlie McCarthy & Edgar Bergen on the Chase & Sanborn program tonight. It was after Charlie had a flying lesson -- and we almost wept with laughing. Charlie spoke in one place about his trans-continental trip and said he'd had mushrooms under glass, etc. but it was the first time he'd had oatmeal over Omaha. Hope you heard it.

We took in $112 at our Fri. nite Carnival but I imagine the expenses were quite high. We gave our puppet show twice, and it wore me out. I have been lazy all weekend.

Myrtle

Hotel Vendome, Mpls
Nov 10/37

Wife & Myrtle,

Things are rotten in my line. Labor takes the heart out of business, seems impossible to close anything. More trouble with the Ford Coach, this time rear end. Cost $55.70 and no money.

The timber strike is causing a lot of hard ship in the north.

I am working on a deal with C.O. Lundquist in Iowa that may pan out. Ole Olson at Palisade bank is to finance it.

Dad

LaPorte
Nov 24-37

My Dear Son,

Friestad's are looking for Myrtle and I on Thanksgiving. I presume your Father will go too seeing it's his folks.

I went over to see Flora last night. I find best way to entertain her is to start her on her latest ills. You see she is what Myrtle calls a person enjoying poor health!

I hear and read so much crazy stuff I fear for the world and our country. I surely hope God will watch out for us for it's certain if he does not we are goners. I see a general tendency to centralize all government and that is bad as it is easier for a dictator to get control. Your Father fought against it but the communists kicked him out. I hope gov't listens to warnings about pulling England's chestnuts out of fire.

I was thinking other day of when you were a little boy time you told me we lived at Tamarack, Minn., you called it "Min". I can still see you at lake going in and out of water all day but with a dirty face unless I got after you. I used to tell you you must fear water on your face would injure you! The farm, old goats, ponies, and so on. How I wish I could go back to that time.

Mom & Myrtle

P.S. Dad still feeling bum. Over does himself and his heart acts up. Still determined to go after C.O. Lundquist deal.

Minnesota Mortgage Company
Waterloo, Iowa
Jan. 6th. 1938.

Dear C.O.

I got here as expected and have started a few adds. Haven't ordered the promotional blotters yet as have not had time to get the dope out yet. I have the Lights and Tel. in so it looks more like an office.

Have had some interest. One has a house for trade and the other is a cash buyer.

Will have to try to find a cheaper place to stay, but can't get any kind of rates in the cheaper hotels.

Marcus

Waterloo
January 12th, 1938.

C.O. -

Ole has me worried. He seems to be swinging into reverse on the deal and never writes, so I do not know what he has in mind. He is a fine fellow, and honest, but others have told me he gets cold, without notice. He being a banker, expects daily results, you and I of course know that such a thing is impossible.

Yesterday I distributed four thousand blotters, which I hope will create some interest. I am sure we will close a property soon and when we do it will take the strain off. Room rent is due, etc. so you know how I feel.

Marcus

C.O. Lundquist, Mpls
January 16, 1938

Marcus,

A letter went forward to you from Mr. Ben Hassman of Aitkin Bank, which looked big enough to include a bunch of cheques. You certainly would not want to have a cheque come back on you while operating at Waterloo.

C.O.L.

Hotel Vendome, Mpls
Jan. 20, 1938

C/O Commercial Bldg.
Waterloo, Iowa
Mr. Nelson:
    We now have three checks of yours totaling $46.25 from Cashier Olson at the Palisade State Bank returned for Not Sufficient Funds. We expect you to take care of these promptly and let us hear from you at once.
    C. Henry Chadbourne, Manager
P.S. What da h--l?
      Henry

Waterloo
Jan. 21st. 1938

C.O. -
    I inclose letter from Vendome Hotel, showing what Ole done regarding checks. He returned them all, so you can see what I worried about.
    Will you call Henry up and talk to him so that he knows that not only am I working on it but sick about the thing, and that he should return them to see if they would not clear.
    They have been so good to me and always taken such wonderfull care of me that I want to express just how I feel about the thing.
    You being more or less a diplomat, can take the sting off. I hate to trouble you with this, but I am.
    Marcus

Palisade State Bank
Jan. 21, 1938

Say Marcus, what are you trying to do to me. Draw no more checks. I must know what is going on. I see no results and looks like there won't be any.
    Ole Olson, Cashier

Waterloo
Jan. 22nd. 1938

C.O. -
    Ole finally managed to scribble me 3 lines and said there will be no money. All that time and he leaves me hung out to dry. I of course am worried sick, but hate to run. I have been laid up more or less the last two days with my heart, no sleep but feel some better today.
    Marcus

Waterloo
Jan 25/38

Myrtle & Wife,
    Stormy here today nobody around. Roads impossible. Many prospects have wanted to go north to look at property but can't get out.
    I have been fighting my heart for a week. Can't sleep, seem to choke up, feel weak. I think the climate here is the cause of up set.
    They say the good die young so I suppose will have to expect mine early. Heard from T-K Mrs. Miller died. Suppose Mrs. Ed Douglas will be next.
    Will stick it out here as long as I can. Haven't smoked much the last week so guess I will quit, while I am going so slow.
    Have recruited a young assistant name of Charlie Laurie with notion of him earning commissions but I wonder how long he will stick on one free lunch?
    Will write more tales tomorrow.
    Dad

Seattle, Wash.
Feb 19, 1938

Mom & Myrtle,
    Got a card from Dad in Mpls. Says Aunt Christine has been taking real good care of him and he feels better. I didn't realize he was so sick. Sounds like he is just now able to get around a little after 3 weeks in bed. He wants to try and salvage something from his Waterloo operation.
    Your idea of a new year-around house at Sandy sounds good. All the other buildings on the place are just too old and not fit for older folks to live in through a Minnesota winter.
    Orv

Waterloo
Mar. 7, 1938

Mr. Nelson:
    People are getting anxious to know when you are coming back. Some of the people have been back three or four times seeking information, but they will not continue to do so if they don't get any satisfaction. They have got me to a point that I don't know what to tell them any more.
    I'm almost disgusted, say nothing of being discouraged. There is business here and there is no reason why we can't get our share. No one expects

a sick man to work, especially when they were as sick as you were, but when a fellow makes a promise, it's a promise, with me. I had a chance to go to work at the packing house as a welder but I turned it down because I agreed to stay here & take care of the office for you. And if the landlord don't kick me out, I'll be here when you do come. That was our agreement. Now! Just when do you expect to be here? Honest! No foolin'.

Charlie Laurie

Nelson's Camp
Mch. 11th, 1938

Wife,

How are you and Myrtle getting along? Place here in pretty good shape - Thompson pulled it thru the winter O.K. I eyed that hillside and believe you are right that a nice house could be put up there. What have you thought about how it should be?

I think I feel some better but still quite weak. "I know I have a heart any way."

Marcus

P.S. No choice but to write Laurie in Waterloo to close the office.

LaPorte
March 24-38

Marcus,

I am writing my ideas about building a place for us on the hillside. We do not need much basement, just enough for storage of vegetables and home canned goods, and for a furnace and fuel storage. So I have decided to just make a small one under kitchen. Can better get heat to every part of the house there, without all the expense.

I want to put up the rammed earth house I have been studying. Professor White of Minnesota University experiment station sent to Washington for information and has told me what he knows about this way of building. I told him the kind of subsoil we have and he thought it would work here. Build forms instead of wood frame walls, then screen dirt and mix with 10% cement, and pack it in frames and let dry. They use asphalt stabilizer to make water-proof the rammed earth walls. Gov't recommends after the earth is dry to veneer the outside with stucco. I think will cost, without labor, well, and modern bath, about $500.00 to build.

Want a small porch entry into library/living room, sunk down 18 inches from rest of first floor.

Gives small house a big look. Toward back is laundry, bathroom. Fireplace in middle of house facing into library. Kitchen facing east and a small bedroom in northwest corner.

The fireplace would be of stone boulders as I did with my cabin. I think we enjoy fireplace so much we should not think of building without one. It's fun to sit and watch the flames. And we have lots of wood will save on fuel when only a little heat is needed.

I want to terrace the hill in front with stone. Have a nice neat gate to side of house made of cement & stone to get to back. Flower gardens on the terraces.

I think we can get along for little money. Land is paid for & taxes looked after by children. Can get by nicely with help of a good garden and small fruit, and possibly bees. Marcus, do you remember what you learnt of bees from J.B.?

I figure such a earth house with thick walls be cool in summer & warm in winter. You & I eat in kitchen most time unless have company, then can rig up a table in library. Located next to road so all your friends can easy get there.

I hope to start on the foundation in late summer, if there is enough money saved up.

Mamie

Nelson's Camp
April 21-38

Darling Orvis,

It's been a hard week here. Dad been quite sick but is sleeping now and quit coughing. I gave him soda water to cut the flim. I am about all in waiting on him.

Orvis, as his condition is such that he will have to have his way or think he has to about the new house can you not write him and give him to believe it was all his idea in 1st place, which not far off he brought idea up year ago but has forgot. I can well see how Aunt Josie likes to come alone to her place on Lake Minnewawa to get away from so much supervision, for Martin & Marcus were shucked from the same ear. By the way, you must write to attorney and get rest of Dad's Pine Island land in your and Myrtle name right away. Lawyer wrote of need as are lots of judgments against your Father.

If I did not have this house to build so I know I will always have a nice place to live I'd be dead by now. If your Father had religion he might be reconciled, but he is not yet. He seemed to feel today he not able to do much at all again.

I cleaned up the "Wanigan" this morning. Straightened up his desk. More wash to do. I am determined to build the new house. This is no real home.

Mom

P.S. I am saving money in reserve for house. Told Dad I had to loan it to you and Myrtle.

Marcus' Wanigan cabin. The river bank is just to the left.

Seattle
April 29th, 1938

Folks,

Sorry Dad had to be taken to hospital but you did the best thing all around Mom. I would see this Doctor about his teeth. They should be X-rayed and as soon as he is well enough and still in hospital, they should be removed. He has had nothing but trouble with them for years.

Dad sent me your house plans. I think you should get an automatic oil furnace, put in an air pressure water tank so can have modern toilet and bath. Wire for lights and can either use that wind generator idea or better yet hook on to highline. It can't be too long before it comes through.

Also better get some jack knife carpenter to straighten out the cabin situation. Fix them up so Dad can get a little more income.

Orvis

P.S. Mom, don't worry about the North West crashes. Those are Lockheed Electras and I am flying only the Douglas ships which are very good and safe airplanes.

Mpls
May 5-38

My dear son,

Your Father is gaining rapidly. He had a fine night without any morphine. I had worried about that but Dr. hinted it was only sterilized water lately. Says have to fool 'em, they think can't sleep without it. Are using deep muscle shots in hip for nerves. Something new.

He is so much like he was with me years ago.

Just wants to lay there and look at me like a child looks at his mother. I had planned to go home when he gets up but he says when I go he goes, so I promised to rent a place till Dr. says he can leave.

Dad says no, we would be foolish to spend more money on the tourist business. You see, he says not get it back under his management. He plans on doing a lot of fishing. I believe now he is reconciled to just take it easy and give up business.

If hospital doesn't get all our money we are going to start foundation of house this summer and go along as we get hold of the cash. But I will have to boss job and he agreed. I guess no choice but to live in Wanigan in winter until house ready.

Mom

P.S. Dad blue. Just hinted to me he was afraid he not live to see any grandchildren.

Mpls
May 19-38

Myrtle,

Dad & I are going home to Sandy tomorrow. His teeth are out and healing but expect he won't be able to eat much solid food for some time. We are sure happy to be leaving here.

I was about at the end two nites ago & didn't come to the hospital but went to see "Snow White." Did not tell Dad because he wanted to see it so bad, said I was too tired to leave room. Was such a nice picture, made me feel lot better.

Myrtle, as you asked I wrote Thompson last week and told him where the boat paint was. He was to get them all ready for opening day. Hope he did so.

Dad got surprised when C.O. wrote had a couple of deals go through from his work in Waterloo. He just beamed. Money will come in a couple of weeks.

Mom

P.S. Your Father said his feet had led him where his heart knew he ought not to go. ha.

Nelson's Camp
June 16-38

Darling Orvis,

Dad sleeping and reading past few days. He been slowly getting together a nice pile of wood for

Mamie and Bill Lainen working on the foundation of the rammed earth house.

winter - Thompson I think doing most of chopping while Marcus does the talking.

Dad had company late afternoon Jim Finch & another man from Duluth. I wish they would not encourage him in business. They staid so long I had to ask them to supper. Finally left hour ago.

Dad wants a milk goat for next winter, may be good idea at that. If it's nice tomorrow he aims to set up a chair on the bank overlooking the river. He always was fond of watching the water.

I think I can take the time to hunt up some workmen for the house. Johnny Hamilton said he would come after foundation and earth walls are up to do the carpentry. With the milling business gone and cheap lumber a thing of the past, a rammed earth home looks like the answer to me, so I will go ahead with it. Maybe can pioneer this kind of cheap construction for future, get Tingdale to work it, etc.

We have been doing better on cabins this year. Fishermen like our lake.

Mom

P.S. Myrtle took on an agency to get her another school. She is updating her "resume."

Marcus enjoying a nice summer day in 1938 just a few feet from his beloved Prairie River.

Butterfield, Minn.
August 5th, 38

My dear Miss Nelson -

    I got your name from the school so am writing at once to tell you that I have a room for you at 10.00 per month, dinners 35 cents, breakfast 15. Have had teachers stay with me for many years as we are only two of us in family.

    Mrs. Jacob Brogger

Seattle
8-31-38

Folks,

    Have been flying trips as 1st Pilot & doing very well, thank you. Glad to break the ice; now I really feel like a Captain should. I guess I can consciously admit I am one now.

    Well, I am to be transferred to Burbank in two weeks. Will be good to get experience on some new routes.

```
Myrtle B. Nelson
McGregor, Minnesota

American, unmarried, Protestant

Certificate- Elementary Standard

Grades preferred- primary, intermediate

Minimum salary considered- $55

Education:
        Graduate of West High School, Minneapolis
        Graduate of Two Year Course, State Teachers College,
        Duluth
        Attended Academic College, University of Minnesota
        for two years

Experience- five years
        1 year- Grandy, Minn., grades 5-8 ( taught with
        first grade certificate)
        After graduation from Teachers College
        1 year- Dist. 31, Aitkin County, all grades
        3 years, Bell Horn Bay School, Mc Gregor, Minn.
        Grades 1-4. This is an accredited school. I had
        a contract for my fourth year at a salary of $70.

Special qualifications:
        Play piano
        Teach art, music, penmanship, gymnasium in all
        grades
        Coach dramatic work of all kinds
        Have written and produced three successful
        marionette shows with my pupils.
        Experienced in public speaking and PTA work

Partial list of references:
Mr. O.W. Newstrom, Co. Supt. of Schools, Aitkin, Minn.
Dr. E. Bohannon, President Teachers College, Duluth
Mr. L. W. Case, Head of Teacher Training Dept. Teachers
        College, Duluth
Mr. Richard Ekelund (board member), McGregor, Minnesota
Mr. P. C. Peterson  (board member), McGregor, Minnesota
Mr. Philip Barett (Dist. 31 board member) McGregor, Minnesota
Mrs. A. Gustafson (former board member) Grandy, Minnesota
```

Myrtle's 1937 teaching resume.

Captain Orvis M. Nelson

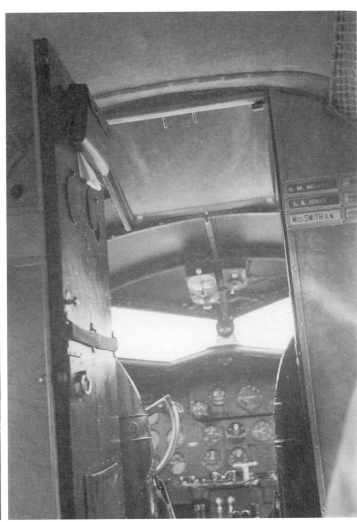

*Upper left, Orvis shortly after promotion to Captain, standing by a Douglas Commercial Model #3 (DC-3).
Upper right, is a cockpit photo of Orvis' first flight as Captain. L.F. Jones was 2nd Pilot, Miss Smith, R.N. was the
stewardess. Orvis' caption was simply "Home". Below, is the DC-3 Mainliner cabin, which could seat 21 passengers.*

Had a card from Myrtle saying she had arrived at Butterfield in fine shape.

Good you have got foundation started on your house. Don't be too discouraged if you can't finish until spring. Some things can't be helped.

Hope Dad continues to gain. Don't let him start drinking brandy or whiskey again in lieu of his medicine. Too hard on blood & heart. Alcohol is a narcotic, not a stimulant.

Orvis

P.S. I'm thinking of flying the Stinson home about 1st of December. I want to fly around the frozen countryside up there once anyway, as Myrtle and I have decided to sell the plane in the spring. Too much expense.

Butterfield
Nov 16th, 1938

Mom & Dad,

Have been so busy with school I haven't had time to think. I like it here - a lot different living in southern part of state. Instead of trees & lakes, they have corn, corn and more corn!

I have been paling around with Marie Harder. She teaches junior high school and, like me, is an "old maid." Her mother seems to be one of the "society ladies" in Butterfield - if there can be such a thing. We were in Victor Brubacher's hardware store yesterday and Marie introduced me to her younger brother, Robert. Seemed like a nice guy - he works at the Butterfield Produce Co., as does about every other person in town.

Orv wrote he is flying the Stinson to the lake first week of December and plans to land on the frozen Prairie River! I must get up for a weekend.

Myrtle

Nelson's Camp
Nov 25-38

Darling Son,

Got word my Indiana house was sold and am glad of that.

Marcus has a rustic bookcase and has been collecting all his books scattered around the country. Has put in his many volumes of the Legislature & Law. Yesterday he asked if I had taken good care of his Shakespeer set and I said yes they were fine and he asked for them to go into the bookcase and I did so.

Dad enjoys so much listening to sacred music on the record player or radio. Doc Snader gave him

several records and he was tickled with them. Thompson rigged up the gas engine so it does not make so much racket when we use the electric.

This morning I was watering the plants in the house and Dad said did you know plants have feelings. Said they shrink in pain when the knife is bared to butcher them. We know that flowers grow so well for those who love them, but wither away from the cold-hearted and careless.

I have been reading up that Heart trouble is usually caused when a child has improper feeding. The Nelsons were given whiskey in their coffee as long back as Marcus can remember, till he was 12 years old and he refused to take it anymore. An old country custom.

Nowadays the young children have lots of school, sports, parlor shows, etc. but never, it seems, any going to church or sunday school. They let them grow up ignorant of God as the way the Russians are doing it. Your Father said he used to think I was too severe about church with you children but he saw now I was not, but had to teach children the way they should be.

Orvis, you should get rid of your money worries and sell your house in Seattle. I just couldn't bear to see you do as your Father always has done in his later years - too close to wall. Ages a person so much and spoils their lives and spoils their dispositions, for your Dad was not that impatient in his younger days. His troubles changed him so.

Mom

P.S. Myrtle sent me some Walnettos candy & I sure like them.

Nelson's Camp
Dec 7-38

My Dear Sister Dilla & Johnny,

We have had just a wonderful time - all four of us together. Orvis came Fri. morning. Buzzed the camp several times and Marcus & I watched him land the ship on the river. Marcus had checked ice thickness and was good 10 to 12 inches and not much snow and so he wired O. it was O.K.

Myrtle came from Butterfield very late Fri. night, long drive. We took all our meals together and Marcus was feeling well - full of pep - and did he tell the tales! Most we had heard before but it always fun to hear them again. Orvis told some too - good talker takes after his Dad. Both of us are so proud of our children.

Marcus told the treasure tale and I had forgotten all about it. Was time we had the steamer "Lee" on

The Stinson

Above, the plane parked next to steps up to the drive camp, taken from the old wood bridge. Below far left, Orvis is sweeping off the wings prior to a flight. Myrtle is clowning around in front of the engine; kneeling in the snow and wearing a Santa Claus beard. Below right, Myrtle and Marcus, Prairie River Bridge in background.

Sandy Lake, summer of 1918 I believe. I and Myrtle was not there but Orvis was, a little boy then. They had finished towing logs to Mississippi and had anchored the Lee in the channel by the Libby dam. After supper Dad got to telling all the boys about time the French and Indian Voyageurs were bringing in an iron chest full of silver and gold crosses from Montreal. The Jesuit priests had converted many Indians and those crosses were worth a man's weight in furs. They got all the way to Libby without incident, so Marcus says, when the Frenchmen were attacked by Sioux in the narrow channel and the iron chest was accidentally dumped into the water and lost. That night everybody on the Lee went to bed thinking about that treasure and the next morning Charley Anderson took an Indian out in a canoe and they started poking at the river bottom with a long pole. After awhile, Marcus noticed what was going on and strolled over to the deck nearest them.

"What is it, Charley, hit something?"

"By golly, Marcus, there is something two or three feet square made of iron down here."

Well, that was all it took for a full blown treasure hunt. They worked all morning to get boom and winch to pull it out but couldn't figure how to get hold of it till Charley Anderson stripped to buff and dove into twelve feet of water and hooked onto box. Sam Rogers opened valve on donkey engine and cranked up the cable. Water boiled and it broke the surface and for a few seconds everyone just stared open mouthed and then somebody let out a wild yell and was roar of laughter. For there, swinging from cable in front of a dozen men, was a rusty old cookstove! Marcus heard later had been thrown over side by the steamer "Oriole" a couple of years before. ha. ha.

Orvis gave Dad 2 or 3 rides just the two of them - flying up the Prairie, Tamarack, and Savanna Rivers. Also around Pine Island Lake. Marcus pointing out all his old camps & talking mile a minute. O. said Dad was exhilarated by the flying, had only been up once before in DC-3. Little plane lots different. O. said when ship bounced in turbulence Dad just giggled - most folks get nervous when that happens (including I and Myrtle).

Orvis let both Dad & Myrtle hold the wheel and do turns and so forth. They about ran camp out of all our gas!

I guess I am going on and on but I have not been happier in years. Marcus & I will finish our cozy new home in the spring - "Beatlands" we have taken to call it - and we can't wait.

Marcus says, "Hallow, all the best to the Indiana crowd."

As ever, Mamie

P.S. Kids are gone and Dad & I are back alone in Wanigan cabin. We aim to loaf away the winter right here.

AITKIN REPUBLICAN
December 22, 1938

MANY ATTEND RITES
OF MARCUS NELSON
AT TAMARACK

Friends from throughout Aitkin County attended the funeral Sunday of Marcus Nelson, well known Sandy Lake resident, who died suddenly of heart trouble on Wednesday, December 14, aged 59 years. He was sitting in a favorite chair in his "Wanigan" cabin conversing with friends when struck down. Mr. Nelson was the oldest living settler in point of residence in the Tamarack community at the time of his death. Burial was in the Round Lake cemetery.

Mr. Nelson was born in Grimstad, Norway on May 18, 1879. His childhood was spent in Chicago and Minneapolis. In 1892 his father homesteaded on Nelson Lake, and the region around Tamarack and Sandy Lake became his home. He took an active part in regional commercial and civic life, serving as county commissioner and state representative. Interested in the welfare and advancement of this county, he had a wide acquaintance throughout northern Minnesota.

Mr. Nelson's occupations included operating a store at Tamarack for over 34 years, logging, lumbering, operation of sawmills, and real estate. He had logged all over Aitkin County, and for many years had a large mill at Tamarack, which was destroyed by the 1918 fire. This was replaced by a similar mill which he operated for nearly 10 more years. From time to time he had additional smaller mills located in the woods where logging was being done. For several years he operated a mill and landing at Aitkin where the drives from the Prairie, Savanna, Tamarack and Mississippi Rivers were landed.

He maintained a home at the mouth of the Prairie River, where he lived until his death. This was the site of his original drive camp on Big Sandy Lake until after the World War. Three seperate mills were also operated on this site from time to time.

Mr. Nelson was also active in opening up the resort and lake shore business on Lake Minnewawa, Big Sandy, Gull, Mille Lacs, Roosevelt, and many smaller lakes.

On May 7, 1901, Mr. Nelson was married to Mamie Barnett of Nineveh, Indiana. His widow and two children survive him. Myrtle, his daughter, teaches at Butterfield, and Lieut. Orvis Nelson, his son, is a pilot on a passenger plane for an airways route in California. A brother and sisters surviving are Ole of Minneapolis, Mrs. Emma Friestad of Tamarack, and Mrs. M.O. Tingdale and Mrs. Christine Foss, both of Minneapolis. He was preceded in death by his parents, a brother Fred, and a sister, Mrs. Martha Larson.

Active pallbearers were Maurice and Ernest Nelson, Haakon Friestad, and Russell Nielsen, his nephews, and Paul Heller, Ed King, Archie Cyrus, Charley Anderson, S.W. Barott, Norman Ofstead, T.B. Thompson, and George Steffer.

Honorary pallbearers were Dr. M. Frederickson, Roy Tiffany, Claude Cline, Charles Lyons, Frank Hense, Tim Mahaney, Carl Lind, and B.R. Hassman.

Texaco Petroleum Products 300 Baker Bldg., Mpls
April 20, 1939

Mr. Marcus Nelson
Big Sandy Lake, Minn.
Sir:
RE: Your Very Past Due Account - $128.15

For the past several months, you have repeatedly ignored our requests for settlement. It has now become necessary for us to turn the matter over to our attorney for collection. Only the immediate receipt of a check for payment in full can preclude this action and prevent permanent damage to your reputation.

Sincerely yours,
Credit Department

EPILOGUE TO THE SERIES

Mamie Nelson finished Beatlands in 1939 (the rammed earth home was featured in the May, 1946 edition of "Minnesota Technolog" magazine) and lived there until the mid-1950's, when it was razed by process of eminent domain to make way for a new road and bridge over the Prairie River. After World War Two, she traveled widely with Orvis, circling the globe twice. The newspapers dubbed her the "Flying Grandmother," in recognition of her willingness, despite her age, to fly anywhere anytime - sometimes acting as stewardess and "ship's doctor."

Late in life, Marcus had mused how nice it would be if Tamarack had it's own "show house." In 1952, in his memory, Mamie built the Marcus Theater, converting the old Koplen Hotel into the Lobby and Projection Room. In 1959, Camp Marcus Nelson became Nelson's Art Colony and Mamie held court in a new rammed earth studio home overlooking the Prairie River. Never without canvas, palette, and brush, she became a well-known regional artist, continuing to participate in family social and business affairs until enfeebled in the early 1970's.

In 1941, Orvis bought back Nelson's Store from Marshall-Wells Co. and opened a second hand furniture and dry goods store. In 1950, Paul Heller retired from his next door Red & White grocery and Orvis bought him out. That same year, Orvis also started the Arrowhead Broom Factory in Tamarack, which operated for a number of years. In 1952 the original 1909 Nelson farm was bought back, and it remains in our family today.

About the time Nelson's General Store put up a new sign ("You Name It, We Have It"), my folks, sister Carol, and I came aboard. Dad and Mom married early in 1942, a few days before he was drafted (and eventually sent to the Pacific). After the war, he went back to the Butterfield Produce Co., but was restless, and welcomed the opportunity to move the Harders to Tamarack. We helped run the various enterprises until 1972 (Myrtle also taught school at Tamarack and McGregor for many years), when fortunes hit bottom again and the family was humiliated by yet another bankruptcy. Fortunately, Mom was by then on social security and teacher's retirement and Dad was immediately hired (in a strange twist) to manage the Wright Co-op Store. He prospered there until his retirement in 1984.

Orvis tried hard to get his Air Corps commission restored when World War Two broke out, but America needed air transport pilots more desperately than anything else and he, along with most of his associates, spent the war in their airline uniforms. He was extremely well thought of in the United organization (he was also a First Vice President of the Airline Pilots Association) and became a protege of United President, William Patterson. However, in 1946, Orvis turned away the opportunity to succeed Patterson in favor of pursuing a cherished dream - the establishment of a new international carrier (United had only domestic routes) called Transocean Air Lines. Just 10 days after forming the new company, he married Edith Frohboese, a United stewardess, and they had four children, Holly, Sue, Marcus, and Jeff.

From the get-go, the upstart supplemental carrier challenged Pan American's Pacific monopoly. The company grew steadily through the late 40's, then expanded spectacularly when the Korean War broke out. At one time Transocean, the first airline conglomerate (ten companies), boasted over 140 airplanes and 6,500 employees. Transocean also helped establish many new airlines around the world (at least sixteen), including such carriers as Air Jordan, Philippine Air Lines, and Japan Air Lines.

Ironically, the company's very success worked against it when powerful competitors began bringing their considerable influence to bear on the Civil Aeronautics Board, whose blessings Transocean needed to survive. Beginning in the middle 1950's, the company was in serious trouble, and by 1958 Orvis had lost control to outside investors.

In the end, Transocean went out of business partly because of over-diversification (Mamie's great fear for her son was realized), but primarily due to the unwillingness of the C.A.B. to grant regular schedule certification, which led directly to the company's inability to secure adequate financing in order to compete successfully. Transocean flew it's last flight in January, 1960.

In later years, Orvis became an airline consultant and lobbyist for deregulation, but fate, as his friend Ernie Gann might have put it, intervened and he did not live to see President Jimmy Carter sign the Airline Deregulation Act on October 24, 1978.

R.E.G. Davis, Curator of Air Transport at the Smithsonian's National Air and Space Museum, captured the sum of Orvis' life with one telling sentence in his Foreword to Arue Szura's 1989 book "Folded Wings":

"Orvis Nelson was possibly the greatest of all airline promoters who never reaped the just rewards of his enterprise, innovation, and determination."

More about Orvis M. Nelson and Transocean Airlines can be found in the following books and publications:

- Davies, R.E.G., *Rebels and Reformers of the Airways*, Washington, D.C.: Smithsonian Institution Press, 1987.
- Gann, Ernest K., *Fate is the Hunter*, New York: Simon and Schuster, Inc., 1961.
- Gann, Ernest K., *A Hostage to Fortune*, New York: Alfred A. Knopf, 1978.
- Lewis, Ralph, *By Dead Reckoning*, McLean, Virginia: Paladwr Press, 1994.
- Robbins, Christopher, *Air America*, New York: G.P. Putnam's Sons, 1979.
- Szura, Arue, *Folded Wings: A History of Transocean Airlines*, Missoula, Montana: Pictorial Histories Publishing Co., 1989.

- Thruelsen, Richard, *The Daring Young Men of Transocean*, New York: Saturday Evening Post Magazine, Curtis Publishing Co., 1952.
- Thruelsen, Richard, Transocean: *The Story of an Unusual Airline*, New York: Henry Holt & Company, 1953.
- Hearings before the Select Committee on Small Business, U.S. Senate, *The Decline of Supplemental Air Carriers in the U.S.*, Washington, D.C.: U.S. Government Printing Office, Oct. 6,7 and 8, 1976.

Mamie passed away on April 13, 1976 - aged 96; Orvis on December 2, 1976 - aged 69; and Myrtle on October 10, 1990 - aged 86.

*Mamie clearly relishing time in the co-pilot's seat. This was taken between
Singapore and Batavia, Java on one of her around-the-world flights.*

STEWARDESS AT 67

OAKLAND, CALIF.-MRS. MAMIE B. NELSON, 67, (RIGHT) JUST COM-
PLETED A 25,074-MILE FLIGHT ACROSS THE PACIFIC TO BATAVIA
AND BACK ABOARD A DC-4 SKYMASTER, SERVING PART OF THE TRIP AS
STEWARDESS. MRS. NELSON, WHO WAS INVITED BY ORVIS M. NELSON
(LEFT), HER SON AND PILOT, TO GO ALONG ON THE SURVEY FLIGHT,
TOOK OVER DUTIES AS STEWARDESS AT MANILA WHEN VISA TROUBLE
PREVENTED THE ORIGINAL STEWARDESS FROM RETURNING. CARING FOR
THE 40 PASSENGERS DURING THE FLIGHT WAS HARDER THAN HOUSEWORK,
MRS. NELSON SAID, BUT ADMITTED SHE WOULD LIKE TO TRY IT AGAIN.
HER SON, ORVIS, IS PRESIDENT OF TRANSOCEAN AIRLINES.

*Edith & Orvis Nelson in Honolulu, 1947.
Edith served as a Transocean stewardess in the early
years and holds a distinction of her own. She was the
first stewardess to fly the Pacific – Pan American used
only male stewards prior to the war.*

Mr. & Mrs. Ernest K. Gann with Mamie on their sailboat at Sausilito, California. Transocean did all the flying for his movies" Island in the Sky" and "The High and the Mighty." After Orvis took this picture, the four of them retired to the ship's cabin for a fine dinner.

Hollywood came to Transocean. (L) to (R), Holly Nelson, Doris Day, and Orvis on the flying set for the film "Julie."

Mamie came into local prominence as a talented regional artist. Here she is being interviewed by Dottie Becker of KDAL-TV, Duluth.

The covers of the promotional brochure used after World War Two.

In 1960, the Art Colony opened. Later there were concerts performed at the camp by the Twin Cities Chamber Orchestra. While all very noble pursuits, these ventures were financial fiascoes.

The finished rammed earth home.
The road ran right next to the stone rip-rap.

1959

HOME AGAIN . . . Back in the school she attended as a child, Mrs. Robert Harder now teaches Tamarack's first, second and third graders. In front row, from left, are Stephen Jackman, Theresa Shofner, Melissa Neubauer, Muriel LeVesseur, Mark Anderson, and Bradley Deuermeyer. — (Staff photo.)

Myrtle Harder Completes Journey: Back in School

Continued from Page 1.

summer art colony at the family resort on Big Sandy lake.

The Nelsons opened Tamarack's first general store, operated now by Myrtle's husband. Her brother Orvis is president of Transocean Airlines and makes it a point to return to his tiny hometown a couple of times a year.

Although the school is older, its P-TA has been in existence for 30 years and recently celebrated its anniversary by mustering a crew of volunteers to clean and paint the basement and fix the plumbing.

Quips Mrs. Harder: "Judging by all the old stuff we discovered in the basement, that was probably the first time anyone has looked there since the school was built."

Now there is an attractively decorated recreation room next to the lunch room in the basement. The two teachers help serve lunch to the youngsters. Mrs. Fern Mead is the school cook.

Mrs. Harder left Tamarack after graduating from its grade school. Later, armed with a university degree, she taught in Estherville, Iowa, while rearing her own two children, both now teen[...]

Kid Cann Case Deliberated By Male Jury

MINNEAPOLIS (AP) — [...] all-male jury began deliber[...] a verdict in Isadore (Kid[...] Blumenfeld and Mont[...] white slavery trial[...] yesterday.

The U. S. d[...] received the [...] instructions [...] Nordbye a[...] rival att[...]

Blum[...] five [...] tute, [...] to c[...] of [...] oth[...]

What Won't They Think of Next

NEW YORK [...] armed ma[...] dope pe[...] $5,0[...] b[...]

Pete Schinn and Robert Harder Sr. in Nelson's Store, Aug 17, 1956.

MAMIE B. NELSON

Announces . . .

THE OPENING OF

The New Marcus Theatre

AT

Tamarack, Minnesota

Saturday, April 5, 1952

Opening Ceremonies 2:00 P. M.
Followed by the Complimentary Showing of Warner Bros. Feature

"FORT WORTH"
To The First 300 Guests
Starring
Randolph Scott, David Brian, Phyllis Thaxter
Additional Showing of "Fort Worth" at 7:15 P. M. and 9:15 P. M.—at Popular Prices

SUNDAY, APRIL 6
Warner Bros. Latest Musical

"I'll See You In My Dreams"
With Danny Thomas and Doris Day
Showing at 2:30 P. M. and 9:15 P. M.

Excepting Tuesdays, Feature Pictures Will Be Shown Daily
Matinees Saturday and Sunday

Swimming near the big rock at the mouth of the Prairie River in 1949. (L) to (R) Myrtle, author, Mamie, Carol, Edith, Holly, Orvis, Socks.

Author at the Main Drive Camp/Camp Marcus Nelson in 1948. I am fleeing an altercation between our dog Socks and another mutt.

The family camping on the Prairie River, July, 1958. (L) to (R) Holly, Edith with arm on Marcus, Brigitte Meyer (the Nelson family nanny), Sue, Carol Harder, Mamie, and author with arms on Jeff. Orvis took the picture. Mamie was hungry and a little irritated with all the photography.

Oakland
March 18, 1959

Dear Mom,

Just a note to wish you many more of my birthdays in
addition to your own. I'm enclosing a little something for you
to use on yourself alone, with my love and appreciation.

I hope by now you are feeling better and that you can
get out and about again. I felt better this afternoon after
talking with you again.

I want you to know too that if I had had the choice of
a mother from all those in the world, I would have picked you.
For after the years we have lived and worked and played together
I am more certain than ever that you are one among millions.
And further, you wear well. You are always a pleasure to be with
and its always a source of pleasure and pride to see how keenly
interested you are in all that goes on and your understanding of
the motivations that cause events and last but not least it is
a joy to see you come up with ideas on what could and should be
done about things, whether at home, in the community, the state,
the nation and the world. When more people in this world have
that sense of public understanding and responsibility than the
world will really be a better place to live in.

Will get up to see you again before too long,

Loads of love,

Orvis wrote this letter to his mother during the dark days of Transocean's final collapse.
I found it in her family Bible, unearthed just three years ago.

110

END NOTES

The letters and documents presented in this book have been edited from genuine letters, combinations of letters, or other documents written by the persons to whom I have attributed them. Except for a few minor dramatic compressions and the clarifications provided below, all the people and events portrayed are real and true.

8/1/26, Common School Certificate: Myrtle's one year of Teacher's College earned her this certificate, which meant she could only teach in ungraded elementary schools, commonly known as "country schools."

8/23/26, Carol Newman: The Palmer and Laurel P.S. refers to penmanship instruction.

10/10/26, Minneapolis Journal: No doubt, there are many individuals and organizations anxious to take credit for originating the "10,000 Lakes" license plate slogan. The May/June, 1996 issue of Minnesota History magazine, published by the Minnesota Historical Society, gives credit to a tourism and marketing organization, the Ten Thousand Lakes of Minnesota Association. It wouldn't be a stretch to assume Tingdale Bros. would have been involved with that group.

12/21/26, Carroll Pitcher: There were lurid newspaper stories regarding the "Daddy Browning and Peaches" affair, along with cartoons of the old man marrying a 16-year-old.

9/9/27, Mamie: Fuzzy White and Baldwin are pseudonyms; she never called the men by name.

12/20/27, Carol Newman: Chilblains was a popular expression referring to the fingers, toes, or nose getting red and swollen from cold weather. The condition was usually accompanied by an itching or burning sensation. "It" refers to Clara Bow, known as the "It Girl" for her portrayal of a carefree flapper in the 1927 hit film "It."

4/15/28, Orvis: During Orvis' furlough, his Uncle Martin Tingdale, who was a mover & shaker in the Odin Club of Minneapolis, hosted a dinner in honor of famed polar flyers and explorers Bernt Balchen (first to fly over the South Pole) and Floyd Bennett (pilot-mechanic on Admiral Byrd's now discredited flight to the North Pole--Byrd saw he couldn't make the pole and fudged the navigational fixes). At the party, Martin arranged for the flyers to take Orvis with them to New York. Unfortunately, a German Junkers plane crashed in Newfoundland and, to Orvis' enormous disappointment, the men flew off to the rescue. Ironically, Bennett contracted pneumonia and died in Canada.

10/16/28, Mamie: Seventy plus years later, that log cabin door still doesn't work right.

12/12/28, Vivian Cyrus: The enmity between some of the "hard-core" first generation Finns and the other settlers lasted a long time. Even as late as the 1950s, I was led to believe "the Co-op store" was nothing short of enemy territory.

1/20/29, Marcus: Mamie's operation was a radical double mastectomy. There were strong indications afterward, which the family did not pursue (the damage was done), the procedure had been unnecessary. One can only imagine the legal ramifications of something like that today.

2/22/29, Orvis: Portions of this letter and several others that follow about flying are partially derived from Orvis' 1942 unpublished autobiography. General MacArthur commanded U.S. Army forces in the Pacific during World War II; Mr. Stimson is best known as President Roosevelt's Secretary of War.

3/28/29, Myrtle: It was all the rage during the early 20th century for nouveau riche Americans to marry their daughters off to European royalty, even if the fellow was suspect.

4/20/29, Mamie: Catarrh was another name for the common cold.

11/15/29, Myrtle: The stock market crashed on October 29th, 1929.

2/1/30, Orvis: Dennis Carr, who never had much money except for his fire settlement, was very generous. It is possible Orvis might have had to drop out of college without Carr's help. My mother once told me, with a faraway look and a catch in her voice, that "he was a good old guy." It was CARR VS DAVIS (Davis was the Director General of the U.S. Railroad Administration) that helped establish the federal government's responsibility for the 1918 forest fire.

3/8/30, Jen: Young women like Myrtle and Jen were beginning to openly discuss such previously taboo subjects as birth control. Despite intense opposition by the Roman Catholic Church, the American Birth Control League was formed in the early 1930's and by 1940 was known as Planned Parenthood.

9/12/30, Wagner: I have oversimplified Orvis watershed crisis of Fall, 1930. After returning to Minnesota, he became filled with enormous self-doubt and was unable to deal with his hopeless financial condition. One morning, after announcing to his folks he was going to quit school, he went duck hunting. While hunched ankle deep in marsh, he began knocking down mallards one after the other without missing a shot. Suddenly, by way of this primal act, Orvis experienced an epiphany. Filled with great resolve - his dream of flying even more intense than before - he returned to Franklin and caused to pass most of the things I have attributed to Mr. Wagner.

1/29/31, Mamie: Marcus and Mamie's relationship was never quite the same after l'affaire Mrs. Williams. There was also a suggestion that Marcus had turned to alcohol for solace. It is possible Mamie presumed the worst (she was prone to make the bleakest assumption), but what really happened I do not know. There is little written evidence (destroyed?), and these are not the kinds of things Victorian families talk about - ever.

12/27/31, Carol Newman: Although Myrtle never spoke about it, I think her failure as a writer always haunted her. In our very last face-to-face conversation, she pleaded with me to try writing again, to pick up the torch as it were. It was her death--the last of the Nelsons--that inspired this work.

Thanksgiving, 1932, Orvis: Pylon 8's are designed to test the limits of every critical pilot skill (except landing) necessary for competent and safe flight. They remain today an essential element of flight training.

12/14/32, Betty Gregg: Regarding Orvis' bachelorhood, it had been a long standing policy that married men were not permitted to become Air Corps Flying Cadets. As far as Orvis was concerned, that was that.

3/12/33, Myrtle: Almost immediately after being sworn in, President Roosevelt temporarily closed the banks of the nation in order to give them a chance to organize their accounts and stop massive withdrawals. The widespread losses suffered by depositors when many banks, like Tamarack's, never reopened led to the establishment of the Federal Deposit Insurance Corporation. On September 12, 1933, Minnesota voted at a special election for adoption of the 21st Amendment, which repealed the 18th (Aitkin County voted 1,906 for repeal and 1,288 against). National Prohibition was coming to an end.

5/16/33, Orvis: Not surprisingly, Orvis didn't write home about the mid-air collision he was involved in on May 5, 1933. Lt. Otto George & Cadet Orvis Nelson were returning to Randolph from Zuehl Field in a BT when another diving BT struck them, nearly shearing off the tail assembly. Hating to allow the destruction of a valuable airplane, they made a questionable decision to stay with the ship and were barely able to bring it down safely. The pilot in the diving BT bailed out and was not injured. A slip (or sideslip) is a cross-controlled maneuver (rudder & aileron applied in opposite directions) designed to quickly lose altitude without picking up speed.

6/1/33, Orvis: Transition is an initial flight(s) to familiarize the pilot with a new ship. Regards the general discussions about pay during this time, it is hard to believe how shabbily the American government treated their most highly trained men throughout the 1930's. Shaky payrolls, lack of flying, and an uncertain future drove many of the best pilots into the airlines or out of aviation. The full accounting, plus interest, fell due on December 7, 1941.

9/10/33, Orvis: Robert Scott is the same Robert L. Scott of Flying Tiger fame and the author of the World War Two-era best selling book "God Is My Co-Pilot."

3/6/34, Orvis: Amid charges of corruption in awarding airmail contracts to the airlines, Roosevelt abruptly canceled them and gave the work to the Army. Unfortunately, General Benjamin Foulois, Chief of the Air Corps, completely overestimated the abilities of his men. On top of that, it was winter and the weather was terrible. The result was an unprecedented string of crashes that rocked the nation. Lt. Colonel H.H. "Hap" Arnold, Orvis' commander at the 11th Bombardment Squadron, went on to become Chief of the Army Air Forces during World War Two and in 1949 became a five star general and Chief of the newly created U.S. Air Force.

3/29/34, Orvis: Orvis told me the 'orbiting the beacon' story one day when we were "hangar flying."

11/8/34, Aitkin Republican: Mr. Alf's platform wasn't much different from Marcus', perhaps a little more progressive regarding beefing up the Income Tax.

12/31/34, Orvis: In the early days, the air line business was largely a seasonal enterprise.

1/8/35, Journal of the House: This description of the events of the first day was derived from the session's official minutes.

1/20/35, Mamie: The "Historical Pageant," like numerous other half-baked schemes cooked up by Mamie and Orvis over the years, never got off the ground. Sometimes it seemed like we were the family Quixote.

4/24/35, Governor Olson: I substituted the actual words "object to" with "veto" to make the action clearer to readers. It is interesting to ponder the which-tax-vehicle debates of the Depression. Today it is only a question of HOW MUCH FROM EACH OF THEM will be necessary to adequately fuel the engines of government.

4/27/35, Mpls Journal: This editorial excerpt discusses the new state property levy of 14.95 mills (up from 11.95). Some words of explanation about the four levels of property tax levy then in use may be helpful to readers. Let us assume, hypothetically, that in 1934 I owned a tract of undeveloped land in Tamarack valued at $500. My real estate tax would have been computed as follows:

Assessed Valuation - $500	
State Mill Rate	11.95 mills
County Mill Rate	63.44 mills
Town Mill Rate	74.21 mills
School Mill Rate	66.80 mills

Total	216.40 mills

A mill is a unit of monetary value equal to one/tenth of a cent. Therefore, a one mill tax on $500 assessed value = .50 cents times 216.40 mills = $108.20 year's real estate tax, or 21.6% of the total value of the land. And this was before the new state increase to 14.95 mills!

There were even worse scenarios - in the village of McGrath the same computation would have yielded it's owner a $222.60 tax obligation! Readers can imagine the enormous impact of this situation. In Clark Township (Tamarack) in 1933, 84.52% of real estate taxes levied were delinquent. The mind reels.

8/31/35, Mamie: Chicago Municipal Airport would soon become known as Midway Airport.

12/18/35, Orvis: While the Boeing 247 had been a terrific improvement over the noisy, ponderous Ford Tri-motors, the two-engine DC-2 transport was revolutionary in that it had variable pitch propellers, which gave it much better performance and single-engine flying characteristics. It also carried more passengers.

2/22/36, Myrtle: Somehow, somewhere along the way, Myrtle learned to speak Ojibway.

10/3/36, Myrtle: I have greatly simplified Mamie's comings and goings during this period; the fallout with Marcus had them both quite upset. I also streamlined Myrtle's life; there was another failed romance and she taught at a little country school near Aitkin during part of the 1936-1937 school year.

11/5/36, Lind: The 54th District sent a series of one term legislators to St. Paul during the Depression. Marcus would have been comforted to know that much of the legislation he supported (e.g. reduction of the real estate tax, installation of a sales tax, removal of the personal property tax) would eventually come to pass.

11/8/36, Mamie: Nashville is still an artist's mecca, though almost Disneyesque today.

12/20/36, Orvis: The DC-3 is arguably the most successful airplane ever built. This fabulous two engine transport cruised at 180 m.p.h. with a 1,500 mile range and ushered in the truly modern age of air transport. There are significant numbers of the DC-3 (and its C-47 military version) still flying around the world today.

11/25/38, Mamie: Reference Mamie's concerns that Orvis not "do as your Father always has done," I have always been struck by the amazing parallels between the two men. Both were big and strong, clear of eye and head. Both were very determined. Each saw great success early in his life; both had a hard time holding onto money and began making the same mistakes: over-diversification, impractical business ideas, and failure to secure adequate financing. Princes when they were on top, there was a tendency toward the "dark side" when things turned sour. Always with the two men, a legal debt was a negotiable item. Each had to endure the collapse of their life work; each died relatively young of a heart attack. Nevertheless, after all is said and done, I like to think that both my grandfather and uncle would still echo something Orvis said when interviewed late in life about how things had turned out for him: "I wouldn't have missed it for the world!"

12/22/38, Aitkin Republican: Marcus' obituary is based on the original published in the Aitkin Republican, with excerpts from the Aitkin Independent Age version, plus factual corrections.

A FINAL NOTE:
Alert readers may recall my previous references to "a projected five-volume series." It was decided to combine most of the original elements of Volumes Four and Five into this single volume.

PHOTO AND ILLUSTRATION CREDITS

- The cover design is by Allison Souter of Chicago. The three family photographs are from the Nelson Photo Collection (N.P.C.).

- Title page photo of fishing boats is from N.P.C.

- 1, Myrtle, from N.P.C.

- 2, Orvis, from N.P.C.

- 3, Certificate and joyride postcard from Nelson Letter Collection (N.L.C.).

- 5, Gull River postcard, Tingdale brochure extract, and newspaper clipping, from N.L.C.

- 6, Tingdale brochure, from N.L.C. Orvis & Pete, from N.P.C.

- 7, Orvis letter, from N.L.C.

- 9, Red Cross letter, from N.L.C. Headquarters photo, by Orvis M. Nelson (O.M.N.).

- 10, Orvis, from N.P.C. Rockwood flyer and Foreman's Report, from N.L.C.

- 12, Barracks, by O.M.N.

- 13, Two Tamarack photos, from N.P.C.

- 15, Parachute photos, by O.M.N.

- 16, Two Manila harbor photos, by O.M.N.

- 17, Cabin, from N.P.C. Airfield, by O.M.N.

- 18, Newspaper article, hula postcard, pennant, from N.L.C.

- 19, Mamie, from N.P.C. Dog poem, from N.L.C.

- 20, Four hunting photos, from N.P.C.

- 22, Poem, from N.L.C. Football photo, from N.P.C.

- 23, Orvis and menu photos, from N.P.C.

- 24, Myrtle & Mamie, from N.P.C.

- 25, Nelson-Heller, from N.L.C.

- 26, Orvis & airplane, from N.P.C.

- 27, Forest Products, from N.L.C.

- 28, Merry Christmas, by O.M.N.

- 30, Fake, by O.M.N.

- 31, Stimson, by O.M.N. Companion letter, from N.L.C.

- 33, Newspaper article excerpt, from N.L.C.

- 34, Missionaries, by O.M.N. Fish note, from N.L.C.

- 35, Myrtle & friend, from N.P.C.

- 36, Ert Nay, by O.M.N.

- 37, Cable & drawing, from N.L.C.

- 38, Air Views, from N.L.C.

- 40, Fraternity, from N.P.C.

- 41, Round Lake postcard, from N.L.C. Orvis & Wally, from N.P.C.

- 42, Tamarack, by O.M.N.

- 44, Two hunter photos, from N.P.C.

- 45, Orvis & Rozena, from N.P.C.

- 46, Four Life at Sandy photos, from N.P.C.

- 47, Aitkin Republican article, from N.L.C.

- 48, Certificate, from N.L.C.

- 49, Letter, from N.L.C.

- 50, Three school, flying photos, from N.P.C.

- 51, Pylon 8, drawn by author.

- 55, Three flying photos, from N.P.C.

- 57, Program, article, from N.L.C.

- 58, Trail, from N.P.C.

- 59, Riverside, Art school, from N.P.C.

- 60, Six cards, from N.L.C.

- 61, Theatre, by O.M.N.

- 62, Mail plane, from N.P.C.

- 63, Fabric, author's personal collection.

- 64, Platform, from N.L.C.

- 65, Nomination, from N.L.C.

- 66, Two puppet photos, from N.P.C. article, from N.L.C.

- 67, Portrait, from 1935 Minnesota Legislative Manual. Bombers, by O.M.N.

- 68, Capitol & Marcus photos, from N.P.C.

- 70, Edited transcript, reprinted courtesy of WCCO Radio.

- 71, Brochure cover, from N.L.C.

- 73, Larson letter, from N.L.C.

- 74, Three bomber photos, from N.P.C.

- 76, Envelope, from N.L.C.

- 77, House letterhead, from N.L.C.

- 78, Boeing postcard and hotel bill, from N.L.C.

- 79, Letter, from N.L.C. Two photos, from N.P.C.

- 80, Two school photos, by Myrtle Nelson.

- 81, Airplane postcard, from N.P.C.

- 83, Four fishing & hunting photos, from N.P.C.

- 84, Four fishing & hunting photos, from N.P.C.

- 85, Flyer, from N.L.C.

- 87, Mamie, from N.P.C.

- 88, Two airplane photos, from N.P.C.

- 89, Check photo, by O.M.N.

- 90, Carr, from N.P.C.

- 95, Wanigan, from N.P.C.

- 96, Marcus and building, from N.P.C.

- 97, Resume, from N.L.C.

- 98, Three Capt. Nelson photos, from N.P.C.

- 100, Three Stinson photos, from N.P.C.

- 105, Three flying photos, from N.P.C.

- 106, Two celebrity photos, from N.P.C. Gann photo by O.M.N.

- 107, Three promo illustrations, from N.L.C.

- 108, Two photos, from N.P.C. Article excerpt and flyer, from N.L.C.

- 109, Three lake photos, from N.P.C.

- 110, Orvis letter, from N.L.C.

Special Acknowledgement

I would like to extend my deep appreciation to Jerry Rosnau, former Director of the Aitkin County Historical Society. Jerry was instrumental in bringing this project to reality. He conceived the overall concept of a multi-volume work that brought together a natural marriage of text and illustrations. Additionally, he remained constantly involved in all the many production and marketing challenges one invariably faces in an effort of this sort. In short, without Jerry Rosnau, "A Minnesota Remembrance" would never have happened.

BIBLIOGRAPHY

- *Aitkin Independent Age,* 1925-1938, weekly newspaper, St. Paul: Minnesota Historical Society microfilm files.
- *Aitkin Republican,* 1925-1938, weekly newspaper, St. Paul: Minnesota Historical Society microfilm files.
- Crabb, Richard, *Radio's Beautiful Day,* Carpentersville, Illinois: Crossroads Communications, 1982.
- Griffith, Richard and Mayer, Arthur, *The Movies: The Sixty-Year Story,* London: Spring Books, 1964.
- Holm, Mike, Secretary of State, *The Legislative Manual of the State of Minnesota:* 1937, Minneapolis: McGill Lithograph Co.
- *Journal of the House of the Forty-Ninth Session of the Legislature of the State of Minnesota,* Saint Paul, Minnesota: Perkins-Tracy, State Printers, 1935.
- *Minneapolis Journal, daily newspaper, 1926,* St. Paul: Minnesota Historical Society microfilm files.
- *Minneapolis Tribune, daily newspaper, 1935,* St. Paul: Minnesota Historical Society microfilm files.
- Nelson, Marcus & Mamie, *family and business letter collection.*
- Nelson, Marcus, *political papers and documents,* 1934-1936.
- Nelson, Mamie, *photograph and illustration collection.*
- Nelson, Orvis M., *unpublished autobiography,* 441 typewritten pages, 1942.
- Palmer, Henry R., *This Was Air Travel,* New York: Bonanza Books, 1962.
- Taylor, John and Munson, Kenneth, *History of Aviation,* New York: Crown Publishers, Inc.,

VALEDICTION

"[Marcus] made it very clear to me that his one ambition was to make Tamarack the best and busiest little town on the Northern Pacific between Duluth and Staples."
   - Herb Colmer, Nelson Store clerk, late in life

"But as we sit here talking we still all agree that Marcus Nelson did the most and had everybody's welfare at heart. He bought the wood products that we had to sell, created work for everyone interested, and ran a store where we could get our provisions whether or not we had money to pay for them. He urged everyone to open up land and prepare farms.
   - Pat "The Fiddler" Barott, 1945

"Tamarack to me means everything. I love all of it including every old timer living or dead."
   - Marcus Nelson, 1931